The
Ex-Muslim's Guide to Christianity

Kenza Haddock

R SE
PUBLISHING

The Ex-Muslim's Guide to Christianity
Copyright © 2024 Kenza Haddock
Published by Rose Publishing
An imprint of Tyndale House Ministries
Carol Stream, Illinois
www.hendricksonrose.com

ISBN: 978-1-4964-8776-6

Appendix by Eric N. Pement, MDiv, MBA.

Library of Congress Catalog Control Number: 2023946397

Printed in the United States of America.
011023VP

This book is dedicated to my Heavenly Father, thank you for calling me out of the pit of despair into life eternal with You.

I also dedicate this book to ex-Muslims all around the world, who took a leap of faith out of their comfort zone, toward the redeemer of their soul. May God show Himself Mighty on your behalf!

Contents

Preface

This book was written for Muslims who have converted to Christianity. As a former Muslim myself, I presume that you will already have an understanding of Islam, its practices, and its culture.

I know that Christians who have never been Muslim will "listen in" to help their ex-Muslim friends adjust to their new life in Christ. If this is you, here's how to say some common words. The religion is called *Islam*, pronounced "iz-LAHM." Followers of Islam are called *Muslims*. Their name for God is *Allah* (pronounced "ah-LAH"), but their ideas about God are distorted. The word *Qur'an* should be pronounced "koor-AHN" (not "kor-ANN").

For both types of readers, I have added a sidebar here and there to elaborate some ideas that didn't fit well into the text, but still might need to be explained.

Also, the Bible is the Word of God, and it is life to me, so when I quote from it, I put it in *italic type,* so it stands out.

If you would like to follow my story more closely, please visit me at:

www.kenzahaddock.com

www.facebook.com/kenzahaddock

CHAPTER 1

From Death to Life

*In the last days, God says, I will pour out my Spirit on all
people. Your sons and daughters will prophesy,
your young men will see visions, your old men
will dream dreams.*

Acts 2:17

I was raised in an Islamic household in Morocco. Like you, I believed I was Muslim from birth, because Allah willed it that way. We were taught that all children are "born Muslim" by nature.

I grew up believing that I had the capacity to "achieve" salvation by satisfying the five Pillars of Islam. The Islamic confession, (1) the *shahada*, was whispered in my ears the day I was born: "There is no God but Allah, and Muhammad is the messenger of Allah." I said it in Arabic regularly. Those who taught that God has a "son" were the worst of blasphemers. I believed that if I (2) prayed regularly, five times each day facing Mecca, (3) fasted correctly in the month of Ramadan, (4) gave enough money to the poor, and (5) traveled to Mecca to participate in the pilgrimage activities at least once in my life, then maybe I could "achieve" my way to heaven.

When I was twelve, my family and I moved from Morocco to the United States. Before our move, I had little exposure to Christianity. I was a child when our family visited Spain prior to relocating to the US, and I remember evangelists trying to hand Bibles to me, and my parents would intervene. My parents taught me that Christians mistakenly think Jesus was crucified and he actually wasn't. I was taught that Jews were hated by Allah, and they were all destined for hell, all of which is based on what the Qur'an taught.

I grew up fearing Allah. I saw him as a god who was closely scrutinizing me, so I tried my best to strive to earn his favor. I was the first of my brothers and sisters to read the entire Qur'an during the month of Ramadan. I made sure to fulfill the five obligatory prayers, plus the additional two. When I became of age to fast, I fasted extra, prayed extra, and carried the Qur'an with me, all in an attempt to gain favor with Allah. However, I could never be sure.

I grew up expecting that negative circumstances in my life would come as punishments for my sins and failures. God even told the angels to be angry with me. One of the sacred hadith was especially troubling. As you know, a *hadith* is a record or narration involving Muhammad's life or sayings, but the sacred hadith (*hadith qudsi*) are a special type. They carry more weight because they are supposedly a direct revelation of God in the words of Muhammad, one notch below the Qur'an. One of them says:

> If Allah has abhorred a servant [of His], He calls Gabriel and says: I abhor So-and-so, therefore abhor him. So Gabriel abhors him. Then he [Gabriel] calls out to the inhabitants of heaven: Allah abhors So-and-so, therefore abhor him. He said: So they abhor him, and abhorrence is established for him on earth.[1]

Based on this belief and after growing up in a traumatic home, by the time I was twenty-three I was convinced God hated me. It didn't matter how much I prayed. It didn't matter how much of the Qur'an I read or how many times I went to the mosque or how many good deeds I did—nothing in my life got better. I was stuck in a cycle of anxiety and depression.

On October 19, 2012, I was so depressed that I bought bottles of NyQuil and contemplated ending my life. That night, a fear came over me. I suddenly knew that if I did go through with suicide, I would end up in hell forever. I skipped all of the Islamic bathing rituals I was used to completing prior to prayer, and I threw myself on the ground, crying. I cried out to God to have mercy on me and to show me the way to him. I then cried myself to sleep.

That night God answered my prayer. I dreamed it was the end times and the heavens opened. I looked up and saw a man in a white robe, descending from the clouds. He approached me, and I realized Jesus Christ, not Muhammad, was coming back at the end times.

On the morning of October 20, 2012, I woke up to an answered prayer. God had answered my plea to show me the way to him. In John 14:6, Jesus says, *"I am the way and the truth and the life. No one comes to the Father except through me."* God showed me ever so clearly that Jesus is the only way to him.

I wish I could tell you I immediately got up and made the decision to give my life to Jesus, but that was not the case. I saw the truth about Jesus, but openly confessing him to my family would come later.

In Luke 14, Jesus describes the terms of following him. Jesus tells the people who expressed a desire to follow him to first "count the cost." This was to ensure that they wanted him most of all, not simply a chance to see healings or miracles. The condition was clear:

> *Large crowds were traveling with Jesus, and turning to them he said: "If anyone comes to me and does not hate father and mother, wife and children, brothers and sisters—yes, even their own life—such a person cannot be my disciple. And whoever does not carry their cross and follow me cannot be my disciple."* (Luke 14:25–27)

Jesus did not use the word *hate* in the sense of malice, hostility, or contempt. That would be evil. His beloved apostle John clarifies that *"anyone who hates a brother or sister is a murderer, and you know that no murderer has eternal life residing in him"* (1 John 3:15). Rather, Jesus knew that following him would be misinterpreted as betrayal or apostasy. If Jesus is Lord, then other people cannot have first place in your life. Following Jesus would separate his disciples from their closest relationships, including blood relatives. Such was my story. Following Jesus led me to cut ties with my mother, my father, my brothers, my sisters, and everyone else in the Islamic community.

If you grew up Muslim, you know how tight an Islamic community is. You're familiar with the importance they place on blood ties. If you change to any other religion, your relatives will hound and pursue you to "revert" back to Islam, because the Qur'an promises that apostates will be cursed and condemned:

> If anyone desires a religion other than Islam (submission to Allah), never will it be accepted of him; and in the Hereafter he will be in the ranks of those who have lost (all spiritual good). How shall Allah guide those who reject Faith after they accepted it.... Of such the reward is that on them (rests) the curse of Allah, of His angels, and of all mankind.... Those who reject Faith after they accepted it, and then go on adding to their defiance of Faith, never will their repentance be accepted. (*Al-Imran*, 3:85–87, 90)

While it is serious to ignore religion and live as a worldly person, it is far worse to leave Islam to commit the most serious sin of all: saying that God has a Son.

The sin of apostasy, especially the apostasy of a daughter, dishonors and brings shame upon the entire family. Dishonor cannot be fixed by talking about "no compulsion in religion."[2] It can only be restored by fulfilling the harsh demands of Islamic law.

Sharia law is clear that apostates should be given an invitation to return to Islam, but if they persist, the penalty should be death. Family members should be the first to carry this out. "When a person who has reached puberty and is sane voluntarily apostatizes from Islam, he deserves to be killed."[3] This is to be done by someone representing the family, but there is no punishment due to the person carrying this out, "since it is killing someone who deserves to die."[4]

During my childhood, my parents frequently warned me of the repercussions of abandoning Islam. After our family moved to the US, it seemed as though my parents became anxious about their children leaving Islam, so they constantly reminded us, "You were born Muslim; you will die Muslim. You know what Allah says about infidels." My parents told me that if I ever left Islam, not only would Allah's wrath fall on me, but it would fall on them as well. A few years before I became a Christian, we watched a documentary about Rifqa Bary, an ex-Muslim who had put her faith in Jesus and sought refuge in a Christian home. Since she was then a minor, she was at the mercy of the court system to keep her away from her parents. While watching the documentary, my parents said that if she were their child, they would have convinced her to come home and then punished her until she proclaimed Allah as her God and Muhammad as his prophet, since Allah has no mercy on traitors.

Growing up, I heard about honor killings in the US, which my parents explained were in agreement with sharia law. They said sharia law was above US law because it was a direct decree from Allah. Taking all this into consideration, when I decided to follow Jesus, I knew I had to move far away.

For safety reasons I decided to move to another state. I took nothing with me but my car. I had nothing and no one but the call of God on my life. And I'll tell you, friends, that was enough. God is enough. Looking back, I'm grateful God allowed me to walk through times of isolation. He was the only help I had and the only one I could rely on so that I could realize he is my Father. Then God provided a woman at church who let me live with her until I got on my feet.

A few years later, I met my husband. When I was pregnant with our first child, my relatives somehow tracked me down and started harassing my husband and me. For a few days, they scouted our neighborhood. A next-door neighbor told us she saw a red car pass slowly in front of our house at least five times, and she thought it was suspicious. I didn't think much of it until the same red car parked in front of our home, and my mother and brother came out of it. We spotted them from the window. When my mom reached the entrance, she started banging on the door, shouting, "You were born a Muslim, you will die a Muslim!" At the same time, my brother circled around to the back yard and tried to break down our back door. I was paralyzed with fear. All I could do was dial 911 and tell the dispatcher of the situation.

While the police were on their way, my relatives tried to open the windows. (Thank God they were locked!) Failing that, my mom returned to banging on the front door, screaming at me, while my brother took pictures of our home, my license plate, and my car's interior. While we waited for the police to arrive, the banging and the shouting on the other side of the door continued unabated. I hid under a desk and prayed earnestly. I repeated the words of Psalm 121:7–8 over and over until the words in my head became louder than the chaos outside: *"The LORD will keep you from all harm—he will watch over your life; the LORD will watch over your coming and going both now and forevermore."* Finally, the police showed up. As the officers took control, I was able to breathe again. The police sent my relatives away.

That night, as I continued to pray, God led me to John 10:27–30:

> *My sheep listen to my voice; I know them, and they follow me. I give them eternal life, and they shall never perish; no one will snatch them out of my hand. My Father, who has given them to me, is greater than all; no one can snatch them out of my Father's hand. I and the Father are one.*

As the years passed, every time a relative came back to harass my husband and me and our children, I stood on the promise in John 10:27–30 that God had shown me years earlier.

My friends, my brothers and sisters in Christ, in this book I want to show you how to stand on the promises God gives you as his child.

My heart for you is that you may escape some of the heartache I went through while figuring out my newfound faith in Christ. This book will help you distinguish between God's voice and Allah's voice. It will help you relate to God as your Father. It will encourage you to follow the guidance of the Holy Spirit, stand firm in the midst of persecution, and live a life worthy of the call you have in Jesus. Best of all, it will explain what you can look forward to in experiencing eternal life.

When God called me out of Islam, I left everything I knew and entered my new life in Christ. I was surrounded by a loving Christian community, which was great, but I had no resources to help me transition from the bondage mindset of Islam to the freedom mindset in Christ. I had no resources that addressed the Islamic beliefs I needed to drop or the Muslim-based thought patterns that would try to creep in.

The Bible says when you are in Christ you are *"a new creation. The old has passed away; behold, the new has come"* (2 Corinthians 5:17 ESV). I wholeheartedly believe that. I also believe it's important to know which specific Muslim mindsets you must consciously resist and leave at the cross to walk in the freedom Jesus died to give you. The Bible says that as believers *"we demolish arguments and every pretension that sets itself up against the knowledge of God, and we take captive every thought to make it obedient to Christ"* (2 Corinthians 10:5).

This book sheds light on the destructive, Muslim-based mindset you must resist and abandon. These thought patterns will especially try to creep in during your early years of walking in Christ, and you will need to consciously cast them down. Then you can walk in the freedom Christ has purchased for you.

CHAPTER 2

Creation, Sin, and Salvation

When Adam sinned, sin entered the world.
Adam's sin brought death, so death spread to
everyone, for everyone sinned.
Romans 5:12 NLT

The account of what took place after Adam and Eve sinned is one of the teachings that most sets Islam and Christianity apart. What you and I were taught in the Qur'an about the Creation and Fall is an "almost-truth" version of what truly took place. Yet an "almost truth" is no truth at all.

According to surah *Al-Baqarah* (2:35–39) in the Qur'an, Adam and his wife lived in a garden paradise (what the Bible calls the garden of Eden) in heaven before the two of them sinned. Then the man, his wife, and Satan were sent down to earth. (The Qur'an does not give the names of any women at all, except for the mother of Jesus. Eve is not named in the Qur'an.) Cast down to earth, Adam repented, and Allah accepted his repentance (verse 37; also 7:23).

Following this teaching has led millions of Muslims—including us—to believe we do not have a sinful nature, and therefore we do not need a savior. As Muslims, we grew up believing we were born innocent, like a blank slate, and that we were blemished by the sins we committed during our lifetime. Yet we had no assurance where we stood in terms of heaven or hell until the Day of Judgment.

Islam taught us that we have the capacity to nullify our bad deeds by performing good deeds to counterbalance them. That's where our "works" mindset comes from. Before Jesus opened our eyes to our need for salvation, we lived with the false perception that we could be acceptable to God by having enough good deeds to outweigh the bad and merit God's approval.

The truth is this: after Adam and Eve chose to sin against God, their sin immediately broke their relationship with God, bringing the consequence of physical death. In addition, a propensity toward sin was inherited by each generation that followed, affecting you and me. Romans 5:12 says, *"Sin entered the world through one man [Adam], and death [entered] through sin, and in this way death came to all people, because all sinned."* All did not sin by personally eating the forbidden fruit, as Paul points out in verse 13. However, Adam is the father and representative of all humanity. All of us are descended from Adam, and all "in Adam" are credited with Adam's transgression and suffer the consequences of his punishment (namely, death).

Maybe it doesn't seem fair that we should die because of what Adam and Eve did. Yet the same principle of representation is also God's way of bringing salvation and eternal life. We have a second Representative. Although *"judgment followed one sin and brought condemnation,... the gift [of forgiveness in Christ] followed many trespasses and brought justification"* (Romans 5:16).

Jesus Christ was the perfect, sinless Substitute who paid for our sins so we can be fully restored to God through him. We were made guilty by the sins of Adam, but we were made clean by the obedience of Christ. *"For just as through the disobedience of the one man [Adam] the many were made sinners, so also through the obedience of the one man [Jesus] the many will be made righteous"* (Romans 5:19).

Just as death came through Adam, so life comes through Jesus. Faith in Christ brings adoption as children of God. *"Yet to all who did receive him, to those who believed in his name, he gave the right to become children of God—children born not of natural descent, nor of human decision or a husband's will, but born of God"* (John 1:12–13).

After Jesus ascended to heaven and the Holy Spirit came upon believers, the good news of the gospel progressively spread throughout the world. In every era, different religions and spiritual movements arose for the sole purpose of slowing down or stopping the gospel. One of those movements is Islam. Islam is not governed by the true God, because it denies the message of the gospel: the good news that God has anointed and appointed his Son to be the Messiah and Savior of the world and has proved it by raising him from the dead.

Islam is one of the devil's tools to keep people in bondage. The Qur'an mentions many stories from the Bible but misses the main point. Regardless of whether the source of the Qur'an is Muhammad himself (hearing Bible stories from caravan travelers and traders) or Muhammad's familiar spirit Jibril (who forced Muhammad to repeat each revelation), the end result is the same: an emphatic denial of God's plan to redeem us through the Messiah, God incarnate. *"For in Christ all the fullness of the Deity lives in bodily form"* (Colossians 2:9).

Without a Savior and Sin-bearer, Muslims are stuck with a phony plan to escape the consequences of their sin by doing enough good works and are deceived by a false promise that God judges sin on a sliding scale. The danger of Islam is that it uses the prophets of the Bible to build up credibility for its own message, and then trains Muslims to suspect that the same Bible is corrupt, so they are afraid to read it and are under threat of death if they leave Islam to follow Christ.

Thankfully, God in his infinite mercy has been revealing himself to Muslims and people in other religions through dreams, visions, or other ways—fulfilling the words of the prophet Joel given in

Acts 2:17–18: *"In the last days, God says, I will pour out my Spirit on all people. Your sons and daughters will prophesy, your young men will see visions, your old men will dream dreams. Even on my servants, both men and women, I will pour out my Spirit in those days, and they will prophesy."* What a merciful Father!

As a Christian, you have a new identity. The Bible explains it this way: *"This means that anyone who belongs to Christ has become a new person. The old life is gone; a new life has begun!"* (2 Corinthians 5:17 NLT).

Before we jump into who you are in Christ and your new identity as a Christian, it's so important for you to know the One you belong to—God—because who you are is found in him, as you'll soon see. In the next few chapters, I will explain important, transformational truths about God the Father, about who Jesus is, and about your relationship with the Holy Spirit. This will help you tremendously as you develop your identity as a child of God.

CHAPTER 3

God's Character Distorted

*I will be a Father to you, and you will be my sons
and daughters, says the Lord Almighty.*
2 Corinthians 6:18

One of the greatest differences between your life as a Muslim and your life now as a believer lies in who you believe God is, and in how you relate to God. When you and I were Muslims, we held beliefs about God that were untrue. The best way to describe how our beliefs came about is through what I call the "character distorted" analogy.

Imagine with me for a moment that you had a profile on LinkedIn. Your profile listed all of your characteristics and attributes, along with references that backed up information about you. Whoever searched for you was able to learn about you through your profile. Now imagine that someone went behind your back and impersonated you by making a new profile under your name. The new profile contains your name, but it holds different characteristics and attributes. So now when people look you up, they don't know which to believe. This is similar to what happened to God's name. God hasn't changed, but throughout the centuries, many have claimed to have heard from God and made allegations about him that were contradictory to his character. These false allegations resulted in confusion about who God truly is, which led to lies spread about his character. For example, as a Muslim, I believed the same God who created Adam and Eve was also distant, mean, angry, and authoritarian, like a dictator. This didn't make him seem pleasant or approachable. In fact, when I was Muslim, I tried to live under the radar as much as possible so that I wouldn't get in trouble with Allah.

The reality is, while we were running from God, he was pursuing our hearts. Although he was pursuing us, there was still something we needed to do: repent. This repentance happened when we understood that before we surrendered our lives to Jesus, our sin separated us from God (see Isaiah 59:1–2). Unlike what Islam taught us, God's holiness is unreachable. There is nothing we can do to reach the level of perfection needed to be right with God. Sin pervades every part of our fallen nature. The prophet Isaiah gives a vivid word picture of this: *"We are all infected and impure with sin. When we display our righteous deeds, they are nothing but filthy rags. Like autumn leaves, we wither and fall, and our sins sweep us away like the wind"* (Isaiah 64:6 NLT).

On our own we were helpless to attain salvation. However, because of his love for us, God sent Jesus to do what we could not do, so that we could stand in his presence and call him Father. Psalm 103:10–13 describes the mercy shown to us by our heavenly Father:

> *He does not treat us as our sins deserve*
> *or repay us according to our iniquities.*
> *For as high as the heavens are above the earth,*
> *so great is his love for those who fear him;*
> *as far as the east is from the west,*
> *so far has he removed our transgressions from us.*
> *As a father has compassion on his children,*
> *so the Lord has compassion on those who fear him.*

In the following pages, we're going to go over characteristics of God that I found specifically helpful as I transitioned from Islam-based beliefs to my new life in Jesus. Allowing the truth of who God is to take deep root in my soul helped me draw close to him and grow in my relationship with him. Let's get started!

Faithful

Every healthy relationship is built on trust. As you develop your relationship with your heavenly Father, you will find that he is a faithful Father whose Word is solid. When God gives you his Word, you can be sure that he will keep it. When God gives you a promise, you can rest assured that his promise will come to pass. We can find ourselves doubting God and his plans for us when we set a time limit on God and expect him to deliver on our schedule. God sees the end from the beginning, and his promises will come to pass in his timing.

As you grow in the Christian life, you'll discover that he is not only faithful to his Word, but he is also faithful to his children. He will not give you something that is not in your best interest, even if you think it is. How often have I prayed for something only to say years later, "I'm so glad that prayer didn't get answered!" God is outside of time, and he sees all of history in a single glance. He sees our future as though it has already happened. He knows what's around the corner of every turn. Since God is faithful to the call he has on your life, he will not give you something prematurely. Your Father knows that giving you that job before your character is ready for it, or giving you a spouse before you work through any residue from your past unhealthy relationships, or giving you *anything* before you're ready for it will just hurt you in the long run, because you won't have the stamina to cope with it.

You may be at a place where a dream is in your heart, and you feel God has forgotten you. You may be at a point where you're questioning whether that dream will ever come to pass. Rest assured, *"God is not a man, so he does not lie. He is not human, so he does not change his mind. Has he ever spoken and failed to act? Has he ever promised and not carried it through?"* (Numbers 23:19 NLT).

Loving

God's love is behind everything he does (see 1 John 4:7–8). His love for you is why you're spiritually alive right now. Coming out of an

Islamic mindset, you may struggle with the assurance of God's love for you. You were so used to a works-based, transactional relationship with Allah that receiving God's love is a foreign concept. If times come when you're plagued with fear—fear of God's wrath, fear that God is mad at you, fear that God has withdrawn his love from you—rest assured of this: because you are in Christ Jesus, nothing can ever separate you from the love of God (see Romans 8:38–39).

As you think of God's love toward you, I encourage you to close your eyes (yes, even now) and imagine your heavenly Father smiling at you with love. Imagine him looking at you the way you would look at someone *you* love. Envision him rejoicing over you, because he does love you with an everlasting love, a love that is both immeasurable and uncontainable.

Merciful

Our heavenly Father's love and mercy go hand in hand. He had every reason to judge us and pour his wrath on us. However, out of his abundant mercy he chose to save us instead (see Ephesians 2:4–5). Whenever doubt comes—and doubts *will* come because we live in a fallen world—remember that Jesus is proof of God's mercy. God is a merciful Father, whose mercy is available to you each and every day. Lamentations 3:22–23 says it best: *"The faithful love of the* LORD *never ends! His mercies never cease. Great is his faithfulness; his mercies begin afresh each morning"* (NLT).

Every morning when you wake up, get in the habit of thanking God for his mercy that covers you. Throughout the day, when you mess up, remind yourself that as a child of God, instead of running away from your merciful Father, you can run to him. The Bible says, *"If we confess our sins, He is faithful and just to forgive us our sins and to cleanse us from all unrighteousness"* (1 John 1:9 NKJV). You're going to see this verse throughout the book because I've planted this verse deep in my soul, as a reminder that my heavenly Father God is merciful. So, when you mess up, run to your Father, confess to him, and ask him to help you walk in a manner worthy of the call he has on your life.

Holy

Your heavenly Father is holy; therefore, he doesn't put up with sin. The only reason we're able to have access to him is because Jesus paid the penalty for our sin once and for all, satisfying the wrath we would have experienced had we not given our lives to Jesus. Because Jesus saved us from God's wrath, we should never deliberately sin, as this grieves God's heart (Genesis 6:6).

If you're a parent, think about how it makes you feel when your child deliberately disobeys you. It's heartbreaking! Sin breaks God's heart. As his children, we are called to live in a way that reflects his attributes. We are able to do this by spending time with him, asking him to change our destructive habits into life-giving ones.

Does this mean we will never sin again? No. *"If we claim to be without sin, we deceive ourselves"* (1 John 1:8). However, we should never take for granted the grace of God and go on sinning deliberately. The apostle John says, *"No one who lives in him keeps on sinning. No one who continues to sin has either seen him or known him"* (1 John 3:6). As children of God, the longer we walk with God, the more we find sin breaking our hearts. As we walk with God, when we sin, God will convict us by his Holy Spirit to restore us. (We will talk more about conviction in a later chapter.)

Gracious

One of the things that used to stress me out as I grew in my faith was "How do I know if the step I am about to take is within God's will?" As you walk with God, this question will eventually come up. Even if you pray about your situation and decide on a path to take, you may find yourself drifting back to old patterns of fear: What if I made the wrong decision? What if God is mad at me for making the wrong decision? What if God gets upset with me for taking the wrong step?

If this sounds familiar to you, let me share my husband's counsel as I faced these questions many years ago: "God is a good Father. If you take the wrong step while trying to do the right thing for God, God's grace will cover you. He will step in and protect you and steer you back in the right direction."

There will be occasions when there is no clear right or wrong answer, where neither direction is sinful, when two choices are open, and both seem good. In these cases, realize that if you sought God and didn't get a crystal-clear answer from him, God is not going to strike you down for making a choice. Whichever direction you end up going, God is with you, and if the step you took was wrong, he will lovingly steer you in the right direction.

Safe

No matter how badly you mess up, when faced with a choice—"Do I run *from* God, or do I run *to* God?"—always run to your heavenly Father. He is the safest person you can go to! The enemy of your soul wants to convince you that God is mad at you, and therefore you should hide from him. That's a lie that dates to Genesis when Adam and Eve hid from God instead of running to him. Don't fall for that lie! Instead, run to your Father and confess your sins to him, knowing that he is faithful *"to forgive you and cleanse you from all unrighteousness"* (1 John 1:9 paraphrased).

Forgiving

God's forgiving nature was displayed ever so clearly at the cross. Because of Jesus' sacrifice, you have access to God. As his child, you can run to your Father, as I stated earlier. I can't say this enough: there will be plenty of times when you're tempted to run *from* God because your old mindset will try to take over. But please don't! Romans 8:15 says, *"So you have not received a spirit that makes you fearful slaves. Instead, you received God's Spirit when he adopted you as his own children. Now we call him, 'Abba, Father'"* (NLT).

If you are a parent, you want your child to come to you and say, "I messed up, please forgive me." When you approach your heavenly Father with a repentant heart, he is *"faithful and just to forgive you."* *Faithful* means God will consistently keep his word, his covenant, and his promises. *Just* means righteous or judicially correct. God upholds his law in forgiving you because the penalty of sin has already been paid; your sins were paid by Jesus, your Sin-bearer.

God is not keeping a scroll of your past misdeeds. That's not how your heavenly Father operates. The psalmist said it best when he wrote, *"As far as the east is from the west, so far has he removed our transgressions from us"* (Psalm 103:12). Your heavenly Father is truly forgiving. Make a commitment to yourself that when you mess up, you will not run away from him, but run *to* him.

Powerful

As a former Muslim, this attribute needs no introduction. You've always seen Allah as all-powerful. However, Allah used his power to control you and bully you. Your heavenly Father, on the other hand, is the true all-powerful, almighty God. He asks, *"To whom will you compare me? Or who is my equal?"* (Isaiah 40:25). Is God all powerful? Absolutely! However, God doesn't use his power to bully you or to put you in a state of terror. Your heavenly Father uses his power for his glory and your good, and he is not capricious or unpredictable, as Allah is.

When you're in a difficult situation or being persecuted, you can take comfort in knowing that nothing is ever outside of God's control. So even when we don't understand what's going on, or if things in our lives don't make sense to us, *"we know that God causes everything to work together for the good of those who love God and are called according to his purpose for them"* (Romans 8:28 NLT).

Protective

In his well-known Sermon on the Mount, Jesus asks that if God looks after the birds of the air and the lilies of the field, which are here today and gone tomorrow, won't he look after you even more? (Matthew 6:26–30). The only reason you belong to God right now is because before your eyes were open to your need for a Savior, your Father made a way for you to be reconciled to him (see Romans 5:8). God is the most protective Father you could ever run to in your time of need. You have no idea how many things, how many situations, and how many people God has protected and shielded you from. Allah left you to fend for yourself. Your heavenly Father didn't want to leave you alone and unguided in this life. That's why he sent you the Holy Spirit (whom we will discuss later in the book) to guide you and to remind you of his love for you every day until he calls you home with him. God gives his angels charge over you to protect you every single day (see Psalm 91).

Committed

Philippians 1:6 says, *"Being confident of this, that he who began a good work in you will carry it on to completion until the day of Christ Jesus."* In Jesus, God shows you that he is committed to seeing you through. God will not drop you halfway through your life journey. God will not give up on you. That's not the character of your heavenly Father. God is committed to walking with you closely. He is committed to guiding you in the path of righteousness.

You will go through times when you don't "feel" God, and times when you wonder if God is still there. That's normal. When you feel God has forgotten you, remind yourself of this truth: there has never been and there will never be anyone who is as committed to you as your heavenly Father. He has not left you. He is with you right now, as you are reading this.

Provider

I could write a whole book on how much God has provided for me throughout the years! God provides for us because he is a Giver. Unlike Allah, your heavenly Father will not put a yoke on you that is greater than what you can bear. The most popular Gospel verse is John 3:16: *"For God so loved the world that he gave his one and only son."* The basis of your relationship with God lies in the fact that God gave you access to him through Jesus. Romans 8:32 says, *"He who did not spare his own Son, but gave him up for us all—how will he not also, along with him, graciously give us all things?"*

When you're tempted to believe God wants to keep good things from you, remember, God is the best Father. If you ask for something that is in line with his will for your life, it will be yours. *"This is the confidence we have in approaching God: that if we ask anything according to his will, he hears us. And if we know that he hears us—whatever we ask—we know that we have what we asked of him"* (1 John 5:14–15).

But what if you ask God for something specific, and he doesn't give it to you? That's when you trust that what you asked for was not according to your heavenly Father's will, and the thing you asked for was not in your best interest, even if it seemed like it from your angle. As you develop your relationship with your heavenly Father, I encourage you to even go one step further: ask God to give you his desires for your life and put those desires in your heart. When you pray, you'll be praying according to his plans and purposes for your life.

Father

I left my favorite attribute for last, because this is one of the most critical attributes for you to grasp as you transition from the bondage mindset to the freedom mindset your heavenly Father wants you to have. When you received Jesus as your Lord and Savior, your relationship with God changed. God is still your Creator; that can never change. But now you are *"born of God"* (1 John 5:1). In place of a *"spirit of bondage … you received the Spirit of adoption"* (Romans 8:15 NKJV). No longer alienated, you are reconciled to God (Colossians 1:21–22). No longer a cowering slave, you became God's child by faith in Christ Jesus (Galatians 3:26). We do not serve Allah in fear but have a Father who loved us before the foundation of the world.

This new relationship erases any fear of condemnation or judgment. Jesus said, *"The Father judges no one, but has entrusted all judgment to the Son"* (John 5:22), and Jesus is our righteous Advocate with the Father (1 John 2:1). Your first few months as a believer, it may even feel weird to call God "Father" because it's been ingrained in you your whole life that doing so is blasphemy. Remember, Islam is based on a distorted concept. If you have trusted in Jesus as the Son of God and your Savior, God is a relational Father. He wants to be there for you. He wants to protect you. He wants to show you and remind you of your worth every single day. And he wants to remind you of the hope that awaits you in eternity.

As we close this chapter, I'd like to remind you that developing a relationship with your heavenly Father is the key factor to growing out of your Islam-based mindset. There will be times when you catch yourself drifting back to legalistic thinking about God. I experienced this for years after I surrendered my life to Jesus. You may go through periods of great doubt. You may be afraid that God is tired of you or mad at you. If this happens, I encourage you to do what has worked for me: Go back to God's Word. Read Ephesians 1 and Romans 8. Remind yourself that the characteristics you are attributing to God are not his, but Allah's. I also invite you to re-review the characteristics of your heavenly Father that we discussed in this chapter. Most importantly, spend time with him in prayer, quietly listening for his response. You'll find that, through time, his love will overcome any anxieties you have, because his love is greater.

CHAPTER 4

Muhammad vs. Jesus

But what about you? [Jesus] asked. "Who do you say I am?"
Matthew 16:15

Throughout his years of ministry on earth, Jesus warned about false prophets who would come after his departure to lead people astray. After Jesus rose from the dead and ascended to heaven, the apostles reminded us of this: *"But there were also false prophets among the people, just as there will be false teachers among you. They will secretly introduce destructive heresies, even denying the sovereign Lord who bought them"* (2 Peter 2:1).

In the decades and centuries that followed, this prediction was fulfilled over and over again. False prophets presented their own "version" of the truth, which was no truth at all. The false prophets were often very persuasive, and as they gained popularity, they led their followers astray. Muhammad founded what is now the second-largest religion in the world, a religion which systematically teaches its followers to reject Jesus as Lord, who bought them with his blood.

About six hundred years after Jesus, in a cave outside of Mecca, Muhammad received revelations from a spirit who said its name was *Jibril* (Gabriel). The spirit told him that Jesus was no greater than Moses, and that Muhammad would be the successor to them both. The religion Muhammad constructed was a distorted form of Judaism, with *Isa* (Jesus) added as a prophet to announce the coming of Muhammad himself.

From the beginning, Muhammad denied the deity of Christ, the finished work of the cross, the resurrection of Jesus, and that

Jesus should be worshiped. The great and powerful God relates to mankind only as master to slave, nothing more. Muhammad placed the yoke of slavery onto people whom God wanted to set free. Jesus said, *"Come to me, all you who are weary and burdened, and I will give you rest. Take my yoke upon you and learn from me, for I am gentle and humble in heart, and you will find rest for your souls. For my yoke is easy and my burden is light"* (Matthew 11:28–30).

Muhammad convinced the multitudes that God, whom he called Allah, is distant, not relational, and requires blind submission.[5] Surah 112 ("The Absolute") condenses Islam into four short verses. Muhammad taught that he who memorized this surah has learned one-third of the Qur'an. It says, "In the name of Allah, Most Gracious, Most Merciful. Say: He is Allah, the One and Only; Allah, the Eternal, Absolute; He begets not, nor is He begotten; and there is none like unto Him." The worst sin is saying that God had a Son or anyone with him in the beginning.

The first verse of several books in the New Testament contradict this teaching of Islam:

> *The beginning of the good news about Jesus the Messiah, the Son of God.* (Mark 1:1)

> *In the beginning was the Word, and the Word was with God, and the Word was God. He was with God in the beginning.* (John 1:1–2)

> *In the past God spoke to our ancestors through the prophets at many times and in various ways, but in these last days he has spoken to us by his Son, whom he appointed heir of all things, and through whom also he made the universe.* (Hebrews 1:1–2)

> *Simon Peter, a servant and apostle of Jesus Christ, to those who through the righteousness of our God and Savior Jesus Christ have received a faith as precious as ours.* (2 Peter 1:1)

Because Islam denies sonship for Jesus, sonship is also denied for Jesus' followers and disciples. In Islam, we cannot be called "sons and daughters" of God, only slaves. Adoption into God's spiritual family is inconceivable—and the Qur'an even makes earthly adoption illegal for families![6] Muhammad removed the most important relationship we could have in our entire life, a relationship with God as our Father. This directly contradicts the Bible, which says, *"See how very much our Father loves us, for he calls us his children, and that is what we are!"* (1 John 3:1 NLT).

Why don't Christians say a blessing on the prophets?

If you were raised in Islam, you know that Muslims give a blessing immediately after saying or writing the name of a prophet from the Qur'an. It may be in English, such as "Adam (peace be upon him)" or "Jesus (pbuh)." It may also appear in Arabic letters or abbreviations. Christians do not add anything extra after naming a prophet.

The Jews did not follow this practice, and neither did Jesus or his disciples. Those who have died in Christ are with the Lord now, and no blessing or ritual can give them more rest than they already have.

Muhammad was very confused about the death and resurrection of Christ. Some verses of the Qur'an seem to say that Jesus will die and rise again (3:55 and 19:33). Two other verses of the Qur'an flatly contradict this, saying Jesus was not crucified and did not die. In surah 4 ("The Women"), Allah puts a "seal" of spiritual blindness upon the Jews for accusing Mary of unchastity and for saying, "We slew the Messiah, Jesus son of Mary, the messenger of God." The surah goes on to claim:

> They did not slay him; nor did they crucify him, but it appeared so unto them. Those who differ concerning him are in doubt thereof. They have no knowledge of it, but follow only conjecture; they slew him not for certain. But God raised him up unto Himself, and God is Mighty, Wise. (SQ 4:157–158)

By far, most Muslims believe Allah took Jesus directly to heaven before he was put on the cross, and some other person, like Judas, was made to look like Jesus, so everybody (including the disciples) thought Jesus was crucified, but he was not. Muhammad saw no value in the blood sacrifice of Jesus Christ.

Muhammad blinded people to God's desire for us to have a relationship with him as our Father, through the Holy Spirit. This destructive mindset drove Muhammad's followers further into the yoke of slavery. Muslims cannot call God "Father," only the unpredictable Judge who gives no one any assurance of salvation. Muslims follow the teaching and example of Muhammad, who was unsure himself whether his revelations were from God (see Qur'an 10:94). Yet, Muslims continue to follow the rules and rituals in the hopes that God will approve of them one day.

Muhammad's false teaching that Jesus was no more than a prophet started a religion that has led millions of people to hell. This is why it's so important to examine all spiritual claims through the lens of the Bible, the standard of truth.

As an ex-Muslim and now a Christian, what I find most disturbing about Islam is that it walks close to the truth in a few ways but also distorts it. The Qur'an alludes to events from the Bible, but with the details vague, fuzzy, or changed. Think about it: the devil lost a big war after Jesus' crucifixion and ascension to heaven. After the penalty for our sins was paid on the cross, those who believe are adopted as children of God, having access to God. The devil hated that, so he inspired Muhammad to produce his own revelations to sway people from the truth—that they have a Father who loves them and wants to spend eternity with them.

Islam teaches that your eternity depends on your good works outweighing your bad works. The truth is, nowhere does the Bible say that sins can be atoned for by good works. On earth, if a person has committed murder, the court cannot let him off if he can point to good things he did. No amount of good works we do can pay for sin. *"The wages of sin is death"* (Romans 6:23). God knew this, and because he is so loving and merciful, God decided to pay the price himself. This was paid by Jesus, God the Son. The Bible says, *"For God made Christ, who never sinned, to be the offering for our sin, so that we could be made right with God through Christ"* (2 Corinthians 5:21 NLT). Jesus was the only qualified person who could pay the penalty for our sins because Jesus is God. Since you and I could never be righteous on our own, God himself came to earth in human form to atone for our sins.

> ### If Jesus was God, why did he need to eat?
>
> *Why did he sleep? How could he be born? How could he die?* These and similar common questions from Muslims show a misunderstanding of the human nature of Christ. Jesus was the Word made flesh (John 1:14), born of a woman. The Bible teaches that God became human (Philippians 2:5–8), not that God became Superman. If Jesus didn't need to eat or sleep, knew all things, and could never be hurt or die, he would not have a human body and a human brain. Humans are born mortal, not immortal. Jesus had to become human to redeem humans. Only if Jesus was truly human could he be our Representative and Savior.

The identity of the Lord Jesus Christ is a stumbling block to Muslims, so in the following pages, I include some of Jesus' characteristics to help you get to know him better.

The Word of God

John 1:1–2 says, *"In the beginning was the Word, and the Word was with God, and the Word was God. He was in the beginning with God"* (ESV). Jesus is the second Person of the Trinity. (I'll talk more about what the Trinity is in the next chapter.) Jesus was there when the earth was formless, and he was there when the heavens and earth were made. Jesus was not created with them; he already existed.

Creator

John 1:3 says, *"Through him all things were made; without him nothing was made that has been made."* See also verse 10: *"He was in the world, and the world was made through him, and the world did not recognize him."*

God in Human Form

Colossians 2:9 describes Jesus as the full expression of God *"in bodily form"* and Colossians 1:15 calls him *"the visible image of the invisible God"* (NLT). We cannot see God physically because *"God is spirit"* (John 4:24). But we can perceive God like we perceive the wind—seeing what it does and feeling its effects. We experience God by the Holy Spirit, and Jesus reflected the nature of God because he is God.

Where did Jesus say, "I am God, worship me"?

Muslims are taught to ask Christians this question to show that Jesus is not God. This is a trick question. Although these words are not in the four Gospels, Jesus said he was the Son of God (John 3:18; 5:25), that we should honor him just as we the honor the Father (John 5:23), that he dwelt in glory with the Father before the world was created (John 17:5), and that he would be crucified, killed, and rise on the third day (Mark 8:31; 9:31). When Jesus was on earth, he was God in human form. Don't let that make you stumble. He was like a king in disguise. He had the same authority and power, whether it's obvious or not.

Authority to Forgive Sins

As you read your Bible, you're going to discover instances when Jesus forgave people's sins. There is a powerful story about this in Mark chapter 2, but that's not the only time. Jesus said, *"Your sins are forgiven,"* and the Pharisees, teachers of the law, were offended by his statements. They were offended because a mere human cannot know this and has no right to say it. They did not see Jesus for who he was, just as you and I did not before the Lord opened our spiritual eyes. Since Jesus is God, he has the authority to forgive your sins and mine.

Our High Priest

In the Bible, Jews relied on priests from the tribe of Levi to mediate between them and God. Each year in Judaism, one man served as high priest on the Day of Atonement. The priests performed sacrifices in accordance with the law of Moses. Since Jesus fulfilled the requirements of God's law (God's standard for holiness), we no longer need a priest to mediate our relationship with God. Jesus fulfills that role.

As a Muslim, you may have thought that your parents and Muhammad could mediate between you and Allah. Now, as I think back, this makes no sense, because the only One qualified to mediate between us and God is someone who is both human and holy, sinless and divine, and that is the Lord Jesus Christ. The Bible says, *"For God made Christ, who never sinned, to be the offering for our sin, so that we could be made right with God through Christ"* (2 Corinthians 5:21 NLT).

Healer

The Bible says, *"By his wounds you have been healed"* (1 Peter 2:24). The healing it talks about in this verse is spiritual healing. At the cross of Calvary, God turned his face away from Jesus, so that he can turn his face toward you and me. Because Jesus was pierced for your transgressions, because he was beaten and mocked, spiritual wholeness is your inheritance in him. *"The punishment that brought us peace was on him"* (Isaiah 53:5). In Christ, you're able to stand righteous before God. In Christ, you have access to spiritual gifts. Because Christ healed you spiritually, you are able to have the closest relationship you can have with God, as his child. In Jesus, you have the high privilege of calling God your *Abba*, an Aramaic word which means "Dad."

Let that settle in for a minute.

On the night that he was betrayed, Jesus reassured his disciples that after he returned to the Father, he would not leave them undirected. He said:

> *I will ask the Father, and he will give you another Advocate, who will never leave you. He is the Holy Spirit, who leads into all truth. The world cannot receive him, because it isn't looking for him and doesn't recognize him. But you know him, because he lives with you now and later will be in you. No, I will not abandon you as orphans—I will come to you. Soon the world will no longer see me, but you will see me. Since I live, you also will live. When I am raised to life again, you will know that I am in my Father, and you are in me, and I am in you.* (John 14:16–20 NLT)

Ten days after Jesus ascended to heaven, on the day of Pentecost, the Holy Spirit came and made his home within the disciples (see the full story in Acts 2). The same promise Jesus gave his disciples in John 14 stands true for us. When we surrendered our lives to Jesus, the Holy Spirit came and made his home inside of us.

In the next chapter, we are going to dive into who the Holy Spirit is and his role in our lives as children of God.

CHAPTER 5

Assigned Angels vs. the Holy Spirit

*But when he, the Spirit of truth, comes,
he will guide you into all the truth.*
John 16:13

As Muslims, you and I believed that throughout our lives, we were assigned two angels: one on the right and one on the left. The angel who sat on our right shoulder kept records of our good deeds, while the angel on the left shoulder recorded our bad deeds.[7] Every time we did *salat* (prayer), we turned our head left and right to greet them. We believed Allah would one day examine the deeds they recorded, weigh them, and depending on which deeds outweighed the other, Allah would decide whether we would spend eternity in heaven or in hell.

This stereotype of Judgment Day traps people in a cycle of "works" to achieve salvation, but works can never wipe away sin. To this, the Bible says, *"For it is by grace you have been saved, through faith— and this is not from yourselves, it is the gift of God—not by works, so that no one can boast"* (Ephesians 2:8–9).

Through the atoning sacrifice of Jesus Christ, you belong to God, and *"he has removed our sins as far from us as the east is from the west"* (Psalm 103:12 NLT). Your record of sin was erased at the cross and erased in your experience when you repented and surrendered to God. Since God is the perfect Father, he didn't leave you to figure out life on your own. Once you became his child, he sent the Holy Spirit to indwell you and guide you into God's will for your life. The

Holy Spirit is such an important Person in your life because he is with you at all times.

There are many misconceptions about the Holy Spirit, even within the Christian community. In fact, I daresay that the Holy Spirit is the most misunderstood member of the Trinity, because we don't take the time to get to know him and how he works.

Before we go further, it's important to know that the Holy Spirit is a divine Person, not a force. Muhammad thought the Holy Spirit was the Jibril, the deceptive spirit that gave him his revelations.[8] No, the Holy Spirit is not an angel or any spirit being. The Holy Spirit is God. In Acts 5:3–4, the Bible says that lying to the Holy Spirit is lying "*to God.*"

In the earlier chapters, we went over the first member of the Trinity, God the Father. The second member is Jesus, God the Son. The third Person of the Trinity is God the Holy Spirit. When Christians use the word *person* in this context, they do not mean someone who has a physical body, but One who has identity, self-awareness, who speaks with his own voice, and is able to love, act, and relate to others on a personal level. Each member of the Trinity is truly divine and is called "God" in the Bible, and yet there is only one God, not three gods. This is the teaching of the New Testament.

The word *Trinity* is not in the Bible.

Neither are the words *missionary* or *omniscience,* but that doesn't mean we cannot use them. By the same token, the word *tawhid* (an Arabic term for indivisible oneness) is not in the Qur'an, but this concept is an essential part of Islam. It is theologically permissible to use a term not found in Scripture as a way to refer to the concepts or teachings. It is the concept that is important, not the vocabulary term that arose later.

The Trinity is active in a verse like this: *"And because we are his children, God has sent the Spirit of his Son into our hearts, prompting us to call out, 'Abba, Father'"* (Galatians 4:6 NLT).

To help you avoid the confusion I went through years ago about the Holy Spirit and his role in my life, I have compiled a list of his attributes to provide guidance as you engage in fellowship with him.

Ever-present

The Holy Spirit is always with you. When I first learned of this, I have to admit, I was afraid. I compared the Holy Spirit's presence to Allah's presence when I was Muslim, which brought nothing but fear—fear that made me want to run in the other direction. The presence of the Holy Spirit is quite the opposite. When you are in the presence of God, fears dissipate. Your heavenly Father is present with you through the Holy Spirit, and his presence brings a peace that surpasses understanding (see Philippians 4:7).

One of the most amazing facts about the Holy Spirit is the fact that he is present with you even now as you're reading this. He was sent to encourage and guide you. He is present with you in the car, where you can talk to him. He is with you watching over you when you're sleeping (see Psalm 121). He is present with you when you're making tough decisions. He is present with you when you're shopping at the grocery store. The fact of the matter is, the One who loves you most is always here with you, not to judge you or to condemn you. He is here with you to remind you that you are his daughter, his son, his treasured possession, and to encourage you in your daily life. Lean into his presence, talk to him, ask him questions. Cultivate the Father-child relationship that is already there. It'll be the best relationship you'll ever have!

Counselor

To obtain wise counsel, you need someone with wisdom. God is the author of wisdom. Since the Holy Spirit is God, he holds all wisdom. The Bible says in James 1:5, *"If you need wisdom, ask our generous God, and he will give it to you. He will not rebuke you for asking"* (NLT).

The Holy Spirit is your wise counsel. As a Muslim, you sought wise counsel from your parents because that's what Islam deemed right for you to do. As a believer, God gives you the ultimate counselor: himself. Does this mean you'll never have to seek wise counsel from people? No. The Bible actually encourages seeking wise counsel from brothers and sisters in the faith (we will touch on this later in the book). God offers to counsel you as his child. Psalm 32:8 says, *"I will instruct you and teach you in the way you should go; I will counsel you with my loving eye on you."* That's God's promise to you. When you need wisdom, don't shy away from asking the One who loves you most. He wants to counsel you. He wants to guide you in the right direction. Isaiah 30:21 says, *"Whether you turn to the right or to the left, your ears will hear a voice behind you, saying, 'This is the way; walk in it.'"*

God is interested in every detail of your life because he has your best interest at heart. Don't ever think that whatever decision you're about to make doesn't qualify as "important enough" for God to notice. You matter to God; therefore, your decisions matter to God. He is here with you. All you have to do is ask.

Comforter

Islam offered no comfort to us. We had to fend for ourselves. As a child of God, you never have to worry about this. I truly believe that as you are leaving Islam, you're going to lean into this attribute of the Holy Spirit the most.

When I left Islam, I left a religion that brought me much anxiety and depression, but I also left everything I ever knew. On the one hand, the anxiety of submitting to Allah was gone; but on the other hand, having to adjust to life with no mother, no father, no brother, no sister, and no relatives to lean on, brought its own type of anxiety.

My *eternal* life was secure, but my *earthly* life felt shaken to its core. Not that my family offered much comfort to me growing up; but having to leave them entirely (for my own safety) was frightening.

Looking back, I believe God draws us toward solitude to show us who he truly is. Sometimes God will pull you out of the crowd. You'll feel alone, only to discover he is your source of comfort and strength. God removed my false sense of security. It wasn't easy, and many times I felt crippling anxiety coming over me. But I was not alone; God was right there with me. I tell you this to let you know that I have lived it.

If this is where you are, press into the Holy Spirit, regardless of how often you remind yourself that he is with you. You may have to do this many times in the beginning, because before you met Christ you *"lived in this world without God and without hope. But now you have been united with Christ Jesus. Once you were far away from God, but now you have been brought near to him through the blood of Christ"* (Ephesians 2:12–13 NLT). I promise you, the more you grasp this truth, the more his peace that surpasses understanding will eradicate your anxiety. *"Do not be anxious about anything, but in every situation, by prayer and petition, with thanksgiving, present your requests to God. And the peace of God, which transcends all understanding, will guard your hearts and your minds in Christ Jesus"* (Philippians 4:6–7).

The Holy Spirit of the living God is right here with you, right now, as you are reading or listening to these words. He is the source of your comfort. He is the source of your peace. If you need an extra measure of comfort and peace, ask God, and watch the Holy Spirit come through for you.

Sustainer

Life is filled with trials and tribulations. Jesus knew this, so he encouraged his disciples before he ascended to heaven: *"And surely I am with you always, to the very end of the age"* (Matthew 28:20).

As I mentioned in the first chapter, after I left Islam, my relatives made several attempts to bully me back into the faith. Throughout the years, they have shown up at my house, they've shown up at my place of business, and they have contacted my friends—yet, through it all, God sustained me.

Early in my walk with God as I faced these trials, I found it important to lean on the promise in John 10:27–29, and as I leaned on God's truth, the Holy Spirit reminded me that I belong to God, the most powerful, the most protective, the most loving Parent I could ever have. The difficulties I was facing were like dust to him. The Holy Spirit also reminded me that, regardless of what I may face, nothing will ever happen to me that is outside of his will.

No matter what you face in this life. No matter the persecution you face for your faith, please rest assured, that God by his Holy Spirit is with you. He will sustain you. There will be times in your life when you don't even know what to pray for. Even in those times, God's got you covered. The Bible says that *"in the same way, the Spirit helps us in our weakness. We do not know what we ought to pray for, but the Spirit himself intercedes for us through wordless groans"* (Romans 8:26). God knows exactly what you need, and his will for your life will come to pass.

Parental Presence

One of the biggest shifts you will experience as you transition out of Islam is about whom you seek first for guidance. As a Muslim, you were commanded by Allah to go to your parents first, regardless of your age. So you went to your parents, your grandparents, or blood relatives who held authority over you for counsel, guidance, and wisdom. As a believer, your default reaction should change. The Holy Spirit is God. He knows the will of your heavenly Father. The child of God should seek the Holy Spirit as their first action. This doesn't mean that God doesn't want you to seek counsel from other people. Obviously, there will be times when God uses people to confirm his word to you. However, it is so important to develop a relationship with God as your heavenly Father through the Holy Spirit and get into the habit of seeking him for wisdom first.

I'm putting so much emphasis on this because I want to save you the heartache I experienced. Shortly after I surrendered my life to Jesus, while sorting through which beliefs were Islam-based and which were Christian-based, I started viewing my pastor as someone who was closer to God than I was. Instead of developing my own relationship with God through the Holy Spirit, I went to my pastor to ask him what he believed God would say. For years, I shied away from going straight to God because growing up Muslim, this was such a foreign concept to me. Although I was a child of God, I didn't act like a child of God, because for some reason, I believed that my pastor was "holier" than me. I treated my pastor as a mediator to God and settled for seeking his wisdom, instead of developing my own relationship with God, through the Holy Spirit.

When Jesus died for our sins, he justified us completely before God. Your pastor should have better knowledge of the Bible than you do, but he is not holier than you, nor does he have more access to God than you have. When Jesus justified you, he gave you full access to God as his child. You can come boldly to the throne of grace (see Hebrews 4:16). Jesus has already paved the way, providing access to the Father by his Holy Spirit who now lives within you! Talk to him. Seek him!

Your Relationship with the Holy Spirit

The Holy Spirit is your divine Guide who knows everything. He knows the will of your heavenly Father for your life. He has your best interest at heart. He knows everything about you, yet he loves you completely. His job is to guide you through life. He strengthens you on the days you feel tired. He comforts you when you feel weary. He also convicts you when you act in a way that is incongruent with who you are in Christ. One of the main roles of the Holy Spirit is to remind us that God is with us at all times.

This is especially helpful if you've just transitioned out of the Islamic faith and are trying to understand the ins and outs of your faith in Christ. God is the perfect Father, and he knows what we need. He sent the Holy Spirit to help us discern his will for our lives. The Holy Spirit will guide you. The closer you walk with God, the more likely you'll be able to discern the difference between God's voice and what isn't his voice.

Suppose someone blindfolded you and asked you to pick out your best friend's voice from a group of people. You could probably do it. Just as a true best friend will encourage and comfort you, they will also warn or confront you when you're making unwise decisions that are not good. The Holy Spirit, your divine Best Friend, will confront you through spiritual conviction.

Growing up believing that bad circumstances were a direct result of Allah's condemnation didn't make the word *conviction* sound pleasant. I spent so many years confusing the word *conviction* with condemnation. Remember, as God's child you are no longer condemned. You are completely loved by God. As your Father, he wants what's best for you, which includes disciplining you when you behave in a way that is not in line with who you are as his child. Does God's discipline mean he is mad at you? No! The Holy Spirit's conviction is proof that God loves you. His voice speaks through your conscience to say, "The way you treated that person wasn't nice." God's conviction is different from condemnation. When the Holy Spirit convicts you, it feels like a nudge in your stomach, and while convicting you, the Holy Spirit offers you a way to repair the situation. This is so different from condemnation, which you are no longer under as a child of God (see Romans 8:1).

Coming out of Islam, you're very familiar with Allah's condemning voice; it needs no introduction. However, you're not so familiar with God's voice. Perhaps for a little while, the voice of condemnation may be louder than the voice of the Holy Spirit. But the longer you walk with God, in fellowship with the Holy Spirit, the more proficient you will be in living out 2 Corinthians 10:5: *"We break down every thought and proud thing that puts itself up against the wisdom of God. We take hold of every thought and make it obey Christ"* (NLV).

Below I have included the most common thoughts you might struggle with as a new believer, along with principles and biblical references to counter the condemning thoughts.

The Voice of Condemnation	The Voice of the Holy Spirit	Bible Reference
God is done with you!	God will never leave you or forsake you.	Deuteronomy 31:6
God is tired of your mistakes!	In Jesus, if you confess your sins and turn back to him, he is faithful to forgive you completely.	1 John 1:9
God is not listening to your prayers!	In Jesus, your heavenly Father invites you to come to him with all of your needs. Be confident that he is listening to you.	Hebrews 4:16
God is not on your side!	In Jesus, God shows that he is with you, and he is for you.	Romans 8:31
God is withholding good things from you!	God has given you the best in Jesus. If he says "no" to something, it's because what you're praying for is not in your best interest. Trust him!	Romans 8:32
God is mad at you!	God's love for you is greater than anything you've ever done. In Jesus, nothing can separate you from God's love for you.	Romans 8:38–39

The Qur'an vs. the Bible

Your word is a lamp for my feet, a light on my path.
Psalm 119:105

Growing up in Islam, you're familiar with the Qur'an in many ways. I remember Qur'an verses hanging on our walls in my childhood home, and I hung Qur'an verses on the walls of my condo as an adult. I read the Qur'an from childhood and even got in the habit of memorizing Qur'an verses in an attempt to gain favor with Allah. This was especially true during the month of Ramadan, when Muslims try to maximize their good deeds since good deeds performed during Ramadan are believed to be "multiplied" and stored toward everlasting rewards (see surah 97).

When we were Muslims, reading the Qur'an was a way to gain Allah's favor. After I gave my life to Jesus, I found myself spending time with God to earn "more" favor with him. I mention this in case you accidentally drift back to the mindset of pleasing God by your works. These missteps will decrease over time, as you discover more about God through his Word, and through experiences with him. Reading God's Word should not be done to earn his favor. We do it to draw close to God and experience his presence. The Bible contains transformative truths that God left to help us as we walk in this life. The psalmist describes the Bible this way: *"Your word is a lamp for my feet, a light on my path"* (Psalm 119:105).

Reading your Bible is so important because it contains promises to encourage you, truths to edify you, warnings to protect you, and exhortations to sustain you throughout the trials of life. As you shop for Bibles, you'll find that there are many translations to choose from. If possible, visit a Christian bookstore to compare Bible translations and editions. My first Bible was the New Living Translation (NLT). This translation is very readable and helped me understand the Bible in its context. Over the years, I have used the New International Version (NIV), the New King James Version (NKJV), and other translations. Whichever you choose, I urge you to find a translation that speaks to you and stay with it. The important thing is to regularly read and digest God's Word.

Versions of the Bible

Don't be afraid to read different "versions" of the Bible. They do not have different books or tell a different story about Jesus. The words *version* and *translation* mean the same. There are many different English translations because people differ about whether the translation should be more literal or more readable. Christians believe God's Word can be understood in any language, and a translation of the Bible is the Word of God. (If you want to find out more about how Christians and Muslims view the Bible and the Qur'an, check out the appendix at the back of this book.)

A Note to Women

When you were Muslim, you were not allowed to touch the Qur'an while you were on your monthly cycle.[9] This rule does not apply to children of God, because our standard of what defiles and what cleanses is completely different from external rituals. Jesus said, *"You are already clean because of the word I have spoken to you"* (John 15:3). As a daughter of God, you can approach him anytime and anywhere, because God doesn't accept us on the basis of external cleanliness, but on the basis of internal purification that has been fulfilled by our Lord and Savior, King Jesus.

The first couple of months of owning a Bible, I avoided highlighting or putting notes in the margin, because writing in the Qur'an was prohibited (partly out of excessive respect for the Qur'an). Christians are more interested in taking God's Word into their hearts and minds than protecting the paper it's printed on, so our Bibles are marked up. As you read the Bible, sometimes a verse or passage will jump out at you, even if you've read it many times before. That's God speaking to you through his Word! Isn't that amazing! When this happens, I encourage you to highlight that verse or passage, and even journal about it, writing down what you believe God is telling you. Do this while the thought is "live," or you might forget it a week later.

Just as God is alive and relational, so is his Word. The Word of God has power to transform your life. *"For the word of God is alive and active. Sharper than any double-edged sword, it penetrates even to dividing soul and spirit, joints and marrow; it judges the thoughts and attitudes of the heart"* (Hebrews 4:12).

As you dive into God's Word, there will be times when God will point out thoughts you have about yourself that are contrary to what he says about you. Thoughts like "I'm such a loser" or "God has had it with me" are not congruent with what God says about you or his own plan to nourish and purify you. When you read God's Word, you may feel him redirecting you. God will use his Word to remind you of your true identity in him.

Use a yellow or fluorescent marker to highlight promises God makes to believers. (If the marker "bleeds" through to the other side of the page, get a different marker.) Stand on these promises as you walk with God. His promises to you will become a shield during spiritual battles. I include some of God's promises in the final chapter of this book. I encourage you to read through your Bible and ask God to show you the promises, commands, and warnings that clearly and contextually apply to you (never take a verse out of context). When you read the Bible later, the highlighting will help you memorize them. When you feel stressed, you'll be able to easily repeat God's promises to yourself, and watch your fear and anxiety dissipate!

CHAPTER 7

The Mosque vs. the Church

In him you also are being built together
into a dwelling place for God by the Spirit.
Ephesians 2:22 ESV

Going to the mosque was a part of the Islamic ritual. As a Muslim, before entering the mosque for prayer, you made sure you completed the following rituals: (1) You had to complete the washing ritual to render yourself clean. (2) You had to be dressed modestly, which included the head covering for women. (3) You also had to remove your shoes prior to entering the carpeted area where prayer was performed. (4) You went to your designated space, depending on your gender. (5) You had to pray facing Mecca, (6) using Arabic prayers from the Qur'an. During prayer you had to follow Islamic rituals of standing, kneeling, and sitting, as postures are deemed important in Islam.

Coming out of Islam, it's so vital to know that your heavenly Father is more concerned with the posture of your heart than the posture of your body. During church service, God is not grading how you're sitting, or whether you went to the first service instead of the second service. That's not how God's kingdom works.

I remember the first time I went to church. Before going, I called a friend to ask what the dress code was. I wasn't sure if I needed to wear black or if I had to be dressed up. I'll never forget her response. She said, "Come as you are."

My friend's response reflects Jesus' heart toward us. As a Muslim, many times I avoided going to the mosque because I was living below Allah's standards. Your life as a Christ follower is quite the opposite. As a child of God, you're not expected to come to God for inspection so he can approve you. Jesus invites you to come to him with your mess, your doubts, with your divided heart, and let him sort everything out. That's the beauty of our relationship with the Father. God does not condone a sinful lifestyle, but I can guarantee you that if you try to get out of a sinful lifestyle on your own, you will do it in vain and go right back to it. However, when you tackle your mess with Jesus, because of his love for you and your love for him, you will find yourself not wanting to engage in lifestyles that are disruptive and destructive. When the truth of Jesus saturates and cleans the ingrained lies you had from birth, you will see how much God loves you and just how close he is to you. He is interested in every detail of your life and is willing to help you. The destructive coping mechanisms you adopted to make up for the lack of love in your life will fall away, because you will be in the very presence of the One who loves you most.

Now for a few more words about the church.

Biblically speaking, the word *church* means an assembly, a gathering of people—and specifically, a gathering of believers in Jesus the Messiah. The church is far less the building, and far more the people gathered to worship God. They assemble to bless and encourage one another, and to hold each other accountable to live a life worthy of their calling in Christ. As you look for churches, you will find that some hold one service on Sunday, and others have two. As I said before, God is not going to approve of you more if you go to one, two, or three church services. You are already accepted in Christ.

Going to church does not save anyone or make them Christian—and you don't have to be at church to receive Jesus Christ as your Lord and Savior. I received Christ in a parking lot! It happened like this: I called a friend of mine, whom I knew believed in Jesus fully, and told him about the dream I had about Jesus. He listened with joy. Toward the end of our conversation, my friend said he believed that Jesus was pursuing me. He read Romans 10:9–10 to me, which says, *"If you declare with your mouth, 'Jesus is Lord,' and believe in your heart that God raised him from the dead, you will be saved. For it is with your heart that you believe and are justified, and it is with your mouth that you profess your faith and are saved."* We talked a little more that night. While walking around in the parking lot, I received Jesus as my Lord and Savior, confessing I was a sinner who did not deserve to be in heaven and putting my trust in Jesus to save me. When I attended a church service some weeks later, out of uncertainty as a new believer, I repeated the "sinner's prayer" to receive Christ again, just in case my prayer in the parking lot wasn't good enough—even though it was!

What about the Sabbath?

Christians usually worship the first day of the week (Sunday), called "the Lord's day" in Revelation 1:10. After his resurrection, Christ appeared to his apostles twice on this day (John 20:19, 26), and the early saints gathered for worship on the first day of the week (Acts 20:7; 1 Corinthians 16:2). In the Ten Commandments, the Sabbath command is not about prayer or assembly but resting from work (Exodus 20:8–11; Deuteronomy 5:12–15). Exodus 31:17 says, *"It is a sign between me [God] and the children of Israel forever."* But most believers today are not Jewish, and the Sabbath command was given to Jews. In Romans 14:5, Paul says, *"One person considers one day more sacred than another; another considers every day alike. Each of them should be fully convinced in their own mind."*

For most people, baptism follows their confession of Jesus as Lord. After you surrender your life to Jesus, you should be baptized (immersed in water), which tells others about the internal change that has come through your faith in Jesus. In baptism, you publicly profess your faith in the Lord Jesus and your new identity in him. It is a visual picture of three things: (1) the burial and resurrection of Jesus from the dead; (2) your sins being washed away through him; and (3) your own future burial and bodily resurrection, which will happen at the return of the Lord Jesus, when his voice raises all the dead from the grave (see John 5:28–29). Colossians 2:12 describes the symbolism of baptism this way: *"For you were buried with Christ when you were baptized. And with him you were raised to new life because you trusted the mighty power of God, who raised Christ from the dead"* (NLT).

Baptism is the initiation or entrance ceremony into the Body of Christ—the whole Christian church. In many congregations, people expect you to attend and participate regularly after you are baptized. If you move and attend a different local church congregation, you don't need to be rebaptized.

Things to Avoid

As you look for a church congregation, avoid cults such as Jehovah's Witnesses (Watchtower), Latter-day Saints (Mormonism), or any group which teaches that all the other churches are wrong except them—even if they offer a free home Bible study.

Also, refrain from churches that encourage worshiping saints or confessing your sins to priests. The system of priesthood ended at the cross, and Jesus is our only priest and mediator. The Bible is clear on this: *"For there is one God, and there is one mediator between God and men, the man Christ Jesus"* (1 Timothy 2:5 ESV). Yes, there was a priesthood in Judaism. But when Jesus died on the cross for our sins, God accepted his sacrifice as the final sacrifice. The veil inside the temple was miraculously torn (Mark 15:38; Luke 23:45), symbolizing that we have full access to God through the Holy Spirit (see Hebrews 10:19–22). The priesthood was transferred from the

THE MOSQUE VS. THE CHURCH | 57

Levites and given to Jesus. Saving faith in Jesus makes you a son or daughter of God. You can go directly to your Father through Christ. It says in Hebrews 4:14–16,

> *Therefore, since we have a great high priest who has ascended into heaven, Jesus the Son of God, let us hold firmly to the faith we profess. For we do not have a high priest who is unable to empathize with our weaknesses, but we have one who has been tempted in every way, just as we are—yet he did not sin. Let us then approach God's throne of grace with confidence, so that we may receive mercy and find grace to help us in our time of need.*

Although God is the only One we ultimately need, the Bible teaches that we should gather with other believers to develop relationships, strengthen one another, and encourage one another. It says in Hebrews 10:24–25, "*And let us consider how to stir up one another to love and good works, not neglecting to meet together, as is the habit of some, but encouraging one another, and all the more as you see the Day drawing near*" (ESV).

Early in my walk with Christ, as I read the Bible I often had questions about what a certain verse or parable meant. You'll probably have questions too, and although the "easy" thing might be to call a friend, ask the pastor, or look it up on Google, I encourage you to not do that. Read the Bible passage again, in different translations. Use cross-references to compare scripture with scripture, and seek God for wisdom, asking the Holy Spirit to help you discern what the scripture means. (Do not open your Bible and flip to a random page. That is asking for trouble, not wisdom!) In seeking wisdom, you may also ask a brother or a sister in Christ, especially older Christians who have modeled a faithful walk with God.

Growing in Grace

God knows that as you come out of Islam, you will likely encounter grief, pains, and some persecution. You will need brothers and sisters in Christ with whom you can talk, share your heart, and grow in maturity. Your church community is never supposed to *substitute* for your relationship with God. It is here to *strengthen* your relationship with God.

When you find a church that works best for you, I encourage you to join a Bible study group. Many churches have groups geared to different ages or different seasons of life. For example, when I was single, I attended a Bible study with other single people. Years later, my husband and I joined a Bible study for couples who have children. It doesn't matter if your church has age groups or family groups, as long as the substance of the study is biblical and helping you to grow in your relationship with God.

At church, you will hear references to "the blood of Jesus." This refers to the atonement for our sins provided by the sacrificial death of Jesus on the cross. God's Word teaches that through his death, Jesus reconciled us to the Father, *"making peace through his blood, shed on the cross"* (Colossians 1:20). Jesus said he came *"to give his life as a ransom for many"* (Mark 10:45).

Many places in the Bible foreshadow the ultimate sacrifice God would provide for the atonement of our sins. John the Baptist, whom God prepared as the forerunner of the Messiah, called Jesus *"the Lamb of God, who takes away the sin of the world"* (John 1:29).

More than 1,200 years before John the Baptist, God established a system of rituals and sacrifices under Moses, teaching the need for atonement and pointing to the Messiah who would provide it. The Passover, the Day of Atonement, the tabernacle, the high priest, the various sin and trespass offerings of an unblemished animal, the priesthood, the differences between clean and unclean things—all pointed to Jesus' sacrifice.

Five hundred years before that, God drew another picture of the Messiah. In Genesis chapter 13, God told Abraham that he would have a son who would inherit the land of Israel. In chapter 17, God promised that Abraham's aged wife would bear a unique son (Isaac) through a divine miracle, and a covenant would be established with him. This sign from God came to pass. In chapter 22, Abraham brought Isaac, now mature, to a mountain as a sacrifice. (As Muslims, we believed that Abraham took *Ishmael* to that mountain, but Qur'an 37:100–107 does not say which son!) Abraham believed that if he sacrificed his son, God would raise him from the dead (see Hebrews 11:19).

These are accounts from history, but they are also God's way of prophetically foreshadowing what he was going to do in bringing about the death, resurrection, and new covenant of the Messiah. When you hear references to the blood of Jesus washing away your sins, these references are a reminder of the price that Jesus paid to redeem sinners, so that we can become children of God—clean, unashamed, and standing in righteousness before our Father.

The Christian church has one recurring ritual for believers, originating in the Jewish Passover. Baptized Christians are eligible to participate in the *Lord's Supper.* In some churches, you don't even need to be baptized, just a believer in Jesus. The ceremony is described in the Gospels and is also called *Communion, Holy Communion,* or the *Eucharist.* They all refer to the same brief ritual in which believers reflect on the death of Jesus Christ. We do so by eating a piece of bread and drinking a sip of grape juice or wine. The Bible doesn't specify when or how often the Communion service should occur. In many churches, it occurs once a month, and children old enough to understand the meaning are allowed to participate in the ceremony also. (You can read about Jesus' Passover and the bread and wine in Luke 22:7–20.)

While these Christian rituals or ceremonies may strengthen your faith and foster closeness to Christ and other believers, they do not, in and of themselves, make you more holy or make God favor you more. Although Communion is a ritual, the Christian life isn't about rules and rituals, but about reflecting the love that Jesus demonstrated for us on the cross. Your new life is what we dive into next!

CHAPTER 8

Old Nature vs. New Nature

Therefore, if anyone is in Christ, the new creation has come:
The old has gone, the new is here!
2 Corinthians 5:17

As a Muslim, in my old nature, I spent a lot of time concealing my sins and shining the light on my good side. Sometimes this meant trying my best not to miss prayer time or fasting extra after Ramadan to accumulate good deeds to make up for my bad deeds. The problem with this tactic is that it's not sustainable. The Bible and experience teach that we carry a sinful nature that cannot be overcome by willpower alone. As we talked about earlier, when Adam and Eve sinned, they lost the connection with God that he originally intended for them. Ever since, Adam and Eve's sinful nature was passed down through the generations that followed, reaching down to you and me.

God knew that in our sinful nature, we would never be able to redeem ourselves. Our sinful nature separated us from God. So he sent Jesus to save us, to redeem us back to him. When we surrendered our lives to Jesus, God put his Holy Spirit in us, claiming us as his. As God's children, he is committed to help us learn about our new nature and walk according to his will for our lives.

Because the Holy Spirit lives in you, God enables you to make decisions in line with his will for your life. When it comes to this new identity in Christ, Romans 8 is such a helpful passage I refer to often. This chapter not only helped me understand my new nature in Christ but also reassured me that in Christ, I am no longer under condemnation.

In the following Bible study, I examine each verse of chapter 8. (I'm using the New King James Version of the Bible.) By the grace of God, you can relate to and be comforted and encouraged by these verses as you see all that the Lord has done for you.

Romans 8:1 *"There is therefore now no condemnation to those who are in Christ Jesus, who do not walk according to the flesh, but according to the Spirit."*

The apostle Paul began this chapter with *"therefore,"* because in the previous chapter, he talked about wrestling with his sinful nature and how sometimes he behaved in a way opposed to his own intentions and desires. Paul started chapter 8 with an encouraging statement to remind you, as a believer, that though you may struggle with some things, your struggle does not define who you are. Your identity in Christ is what dictates who you are. Out of your identity in Christ, God gives you the ability to behave in a way that is pleasing to him. While your sinful nature craves sin, your spirit craves God's desires.

During his ministry on earth, Jesus was presented with a woman who had been caught in the act of adultery. The teachers of the law at the time wanted her stoned, according to the law. But instead of condemning her, Jesus chose to respond in mercy, and encouraged her to leave her life of sin (see John 8:1–11).

Romans 8:2 *"For the law of the Spirit of life in Christ Jesus has made me free from the law of sin and death."*

Just because Jesus didn't condemn the woman caught in adultery doesn't mean that he condones sin. On the contrary, he came to deal with sin once and for all. He also knew that condemning someone into "good behavior" doesn't work. This verse shows that through Jesus, God gives you the power to make decisions that are consistent with the will of God for your life. When you're walking in the Spirit of God, you begin to desire the things of God, and you start to behave in a way that resembles your heavenly Father's character, because you belong to him. You are his child.

Romans 8:3 *"For what the law could not do in that it was weak through the flesh, God did by sending His own Son in the likeness of sinful flesh, on account of sin: He condemned sin in the flesh,"*

Here, Paul reiterates that God's standard for holiness was unachievable by human effort. Therefore, in order to redeem us, God sent his innocent Son Jesus to live a perfect life and die a sinner's death, satisfying God's wrath for sin, forever changing our status with God.

Romans 8:4 *"that the righteous requirement of the law might be fulfilled in us who do not walk according to the flesh but according to the Spirit."*

The righteous requirement of the law insisted that you and I should receive God's wrath due to our sin. However, when we submit to the Lordship of Jesus, we become God's children, and the evidence of this is God's Holy Spirit alive in us.

Romans 8:5 *"For those who live according to the flesh set their minds on the things of the flesh, but those who live according to the Spirit, the things of the Spirit."*

When you became God's child, God placed his desires in your heart. You may find that the things you used to enjoy you no longer enjoy, because your desires have changed. An example of this happened to me a few months after I gave my life to Jesus. God gave me a desire to help individuals who were oppressed and those fighting mental health battles. I left my former career and pursued the counseling field. God blessed this venture. So don't be surprised if you feel prompted to take part in a ministry, or to start a ministry, or if you find yourself feeling compassionate toward a certain cause.

God's Word says, *"May he give you the desire of your heart and make all your plans succeed"* (Psalm 20:4). Many have mistaken this verse to mean that God will give them anything they want. This verse means that as God's child, God will put his desires in your heart. You will be drawn to things that please God.

Romans 8:6 *"For to be carnally minded is death, but to be spiritually minded is life and peace."*

As a believer, every single day we are faced with two choices: to follow the old nature, which is destructive, or to heed the guidance of the Holy Spirit, who is within us and who leads us to life.

Romans 8:7 *"Because the carnal mind is enmity against God; for it is not subject to the law of God, nor indeed can be."*

As Muslims, we were led by our sinful cravings, rooted in pride and a "me-focused" attitude.

Romans 8:8 *"So then, those who are in the flesh cannot please God."*

The "works" mindset we were stuck in could never please God.

Romans 8:9 *"But you are not in the flesh but in the Spirit, if indeed the Spirit of God dwells in you. Now if anyone does not have the Spirit of Christ, he is not His."*

When we surrendered our lives to Jesus and God became our Father, the Holy Spirit made his home with us. He will faithfully help us choose paths that are pleasing to God.

Romans 8:10 *"And if Christ is in you, the body is dead because of sin, but the Spirit is life because of righteousness."*

When we die, our spirit is secure because of our salvation in Jesus.

Romans 8:11 *"But if the Spirit of Him who raised Jesus from* *the dead dwells in you, He who raised Christ from the dead will also give life to your mortal bodies through His Spirit who dwells in you."*

When you left Islam and surrendered your life to Jesus, the Holy Spirit made his home in you, and you went from spiritual death to spiritual life. In addition, we have the promise of physical immortality in a body that will be raised like Jesus' body.

Romans 8:12 *"Therefore, brethren, we are debtors—not to the flesh, to live according to the flesh."*

When sin knocks at your door, trying to deter you from the call God has on your life by the Holy Spirit, who lives in you, you are able to say *no*. God equips you and is cheering you on.

Romans 8:13 *"For if you live according to the flesh you will die; but if by the Spirit you put to death the deeds of the body, you will live."*

God gives you the Holy Spirit to equip you to say *no* to sin, because sin leads to destruction.

Romans 8:14 *"For as many as are led by the Spirit of God, these are sons of God."*

God counts you as his child. As a good, loving Father, he leads you in the right path by the Holy Spirit.

Romans 8:15 *"For you did not receive the spirit of bondage again to fear, but you received the Spirit of adoption by whom we cry out, 'Abba, Father.'"*

As God's child, you are never alone because the Holy Spirit is with you, comforting you, encouraging you, counseling you, and guiding you throughout your life.

Romans 8:16 *"The Spirit Himself bears witness with our spirit that we are children of God,"*

The Holy Spirit, living inside of you, is proof that you are a son or daughter of God and that God has placed his stamp of approval on you, a stamp no one can take from you.

Romans 8:17 *"and if children, then heirs—heirs of God and joint heirs with Christ, if indeed we suffer with Him, that we may also be glorified together."*

This is so unlike Islam, when you didn't know whether you would go to heaven or hell. As a child of God, you get to inherit eternity in heaven with your heavenly Father, who loves you with an everlasting love. This is an assurance no one can ever take from you.

Romans 8:18 *"For I consider that the sufferings of this present time are not worthy to be compared with the glory which shall be revealed in us."*

As I mentioned earlier in this book, the kingdom of heaven and the movement of the gospel has been resisted and fought against for centuries. As a child of God, you are not exempt from suffering for your faith. This is especially true for you as an ex-Muslim. For me, the cost came from my blood relatives, being persecuted by them for my faith. It may be the same for you, or your suffering may look like something else. In whatever way your persecution may come, rest assured that God is with you. God is for you. He will never leave you or forsake you (see Hebrews 13:5).

Romans 8:19–21 *"For the earnest expectation of the creation eagerly waits for the revealing of the sons of God. For the creation was subjected to futility, not willingly, but because of Him who subjected it in hope; because the creation itself also will be delivered from the bondage of corruption into the glorious liberty of the children of God."*

As we stand firm in our faith, we look forward in hope to the second coming of our Savior.

Romans 8:22–25 *"For we know that the whole creation groans and labors with birth pangs together until now. Not only that, but we also who have the first fruits of the Spirit, even we ourselves groan within ourselves, eagerly waiting for the adoption, the redemption of our body. For we were saved in this hope, but hope that is seen is not hope; for why does one still hope for what he sees? But if we hope for what we do not see, we eagerly wait for it with perseverance."*

As we go through trials and tribulations here on earth, always remember that earth is not our home. We belong with Christ Jesus. If you're enduring persecution for your faith, may you stand firm in hope, knowing that you are secure in Christ. No matter what comes your way in this life, your security lies in who you are in Christ.

Romans 8:26 *"Likewise the Spirit also helps in our weaknesses. For we do not know what we should pray for as we ought, but the Spirit Himself makes intercession for us with groanings which cannot be uttered."*

There will be times when you're on your knees, crying out to God, unable to even utter words out of your mouth. In those times, rest assured that the Holy Spirit is with you. He knows what you need and will intercede on your behalf to your heavenly Father.

Romans 8:27 *"Now He who searches the hearts knows what the mind of the Spirit is, because He makes intercession for the saints according to the will of God."*

The Holy Spirit, who is always with you, knows exactly what you need and, at the same time, knows God's will for your life.

Romans 8:28 *"And we know that all things work together for good to those who love God, to those who are the called according to His purpose."*

Whatever your life circumstances may be, always know that God is with you. He knows what you are going through, and he will bring something good out of your circumstances. Always remember: God's will and purpose for your life will prevail.

Romans 8:29 *"For whom He foreknew, He also predestined to be conformed to the image of His Son, that He might be the firstborn among many brethren."*

God's will for your life is to conform you to the image of Jesus. Remember, you are an image-bearer of God. So as you walk in Christ, he will start manifesting the fruit and the gifts of the Holy Spirit.

Romans 8:30 *"Moreover whom He predestined, these He also called; whom He called, these He also justified; and whom He justified, these He also glorified."*

God chose to save you out of the abundance of his mercy and grace. Because of what Jesus did for you, you now stand righteous before God, which is why you have access to God as his child. Regardless of what condemning thoughts may come to mind, remember that in Jesus, God accepts you fully—not just the parts of you that "look good." He adopts you as you are, and by his Holy Spirit, he works to conform you into the image of Jesus.

Romans 8:31 *"What then shall we say to these things? If God is for us, who can be against us?"*

If the God of the universe put his stamp of approval on you, it doesn't matter who condemns you. God is the standard. Although as an ex-Muslim who may face persecution for your faith in Jesus, the God of the universe, the King of kings, calls you his child. If your family shuns you for it, so be it. He accepts you fully, and that's all that matters.

Romans 8:32 *"He who did not spare His own Son, but delivered Him up for us all, how shall He not with Him also freely give us all things?"*

I leaned on this verse so much my first few years as a child of God. Leaving your family causes a security crisis. There were many times when I found myself asking questions like, *Will God really provide for me? Is God really going to be with me always?*

Questions like these are normal for ex-Muslims because your blood relatives are so tangible! When you give your life to Jesus, you learn to walk in fellowship with the Holy Spirit and recognize God's voice. There will be times when you wonder if God truly is there. One of my favorite things about God is, since he made you, he knows exactly how to talk to you, reassuring and reminding you that you are his child, that he loves you, and that nothing can ever separate you from his love.

Romans 8:33 *"Who shall bring a charge against God's elect? It is God who justifies."*

After I gave my life to Jesus, I received emails from family members saying they had dreams from Allah that I was on my way to hell. You may receive emails or letters or other fear tactics after you surrender your life to Jesus. When this happens, remember that the God of the universe calls you his child. Even if it feels like the whole world is against you—and often as an ex-Muslim, your "whole world" is isolated—the only one you need on your side is God. And God is *for* you.

Romans 8:34 *"Who is he who condemns? It is Christ who died, and furthermore is also risen, who is even at the right hand of God, who also makes intercession for us."*

Jesus is the judge of the living and the dead. He calls you righteous before God, and therefore you are.

Romans 8:35 *"Who shall separate us from the love of Christ? Shall tribulation, or distress, or persecution, or famine, or nakedness, or peril, or sword?"*

This was such an important verse for me to stand on when I left Islam—and even now, I still stand on this verse year after year. As a Muslim, you used to believe that tribulation was probably a punishment from Allah. In fact, this belief was so ingrained in me that the first few times my blood relatives came to persecute me for my faith, my mind went straight to "Did I do something to make God mad at me? Did God decide to send them to persecute me because he is mad at me?"

What helped me overcome this bondage was going back through Romans chapter 8 over and over and over, to the point where I have it memorized now! No matter how many times you have to go back to Romans 8 verse 1, then go back to it, and then read all the way through verse 35, again and again, to remind yourself that nothing will ever separate you from the love of God shown through Christ. You'll find that Romans 8 is one of the most life-transforming chapters!

Romans 8:36–39 *"As it is written: 'For Your sake we are killed all day long; We are accounted as sheep for the slaughter.' Yet in all these things we are more than conquerors through Him who loved us. For I am persuaded that neither death nor life, nor angels nor principalities nor powers, nor things present nor things to come, nor height nor depth, nor any other created thing, shall be able to separate us from the love of God which is in Christ Jesus our Lord."*

As a Muslim, you were so used to identifying negative life circumstances as Allah punishing you. That perspective controlled my life to the point where I hyper-spiritualized everything. For example, if I was driving and got pulled over by a traffic officer, I wondered what I had done wrong earlier that day for Allah to punish me.

I am grateful that God included this chapter in Romans for believers to be reminded that he does not *cause* bad things to happen to us. He may allow negative circumstances, and if he does, we can be sure that he will bring something good out of it. As a child of God, you can live your life confident that in Christ, you have conquered the gates of hell. In Christ, nothing can ever separate you from God's love. In Christ, you have full access to the One who loves you most. In Christ, you can rest assured that you will live eternally with your heavenly Father, the lover of your soul.

As your sister in Christ who left Islam, just as you did, I encourage you to memorize Romans 8, because it speaks to your true identity in Christ. Memorizing Romans 8 was so helpful to me when condemning thoughts came to my mind. I was able to remind myself of the truth in Romans 8:1: *"There is therefore now no condemnation to those who are in Christ Jesus."*

The great thing about this passage is, you can even personalize it so you can preach the Word of God to your anxiety and fears. For example, when anxiety was creeping in, I would repeat to myself, "There is therefore now no condemnation for *me* because *I* am in Christ Jesus."

CHAPTER 9

Your Salvation

For it is by grace you have been saved, through faith—and this is not from yourselves, it is the gift of God—not by works, so that no one can boast.

Ephesians 2:8-9

As an ex-Muslim, I'm sure questions like *Why did God save me? What made God choose me?* and *Why me?* have crossed your mind. I have to confess that in my early years of walking with the Lord, I subconsciously or semi-consciously wondered if something special about me caused God to look at me favorably. It saddens me now to consider how long I thought that way. Looking for what was "good" in me kept me in the bondage of having to maintain my good works to maintain God's acceptance.

Ephesians 2:8–9 is clear that God's salvation is a gift that none of us could earn. God's choice to save us was out of his mercy and grace. His choice to save us came from his loving nature, as is shown throughout Scripture. There's a passage that specifically speaks to this matter that I believe will help you grasp God's unconditional love for you.

We will walk together through Ephesians chapter 1, starting in verse 3, in the New International Version of the Bible. I pray that the truths of his Word will take root in the depths of your heart. Let's take a look!

Ephesians 1:3 *"Praise be to the God and Father of our Lord Jesus Christ, who has blessed us in the heavenly realms with every spiritual blessing in Christ."*

I love how this passage, right off the bat, reminds you that God is your Father and Jesus is your Lord. And your Father has blessed you *"with every spiritual blessing."* Our main spiritual blessing is the fact that God chose to redeem us and adopt us as his children. Our other spiritual blessings include the facts that the Holy Spirit is always with us, guiding us, and we have access to the gifts and the fruit of the Holy Spirit.

Ephesians 1:4 *"For he chose us in him before the creation of the world to be holy and blameless in his sight."*

Before the world was created, God knew that you would inherit a sinful nature that could only be redeemed by himself. Before you were conceived, God had already made the plan to save you, redeem you, and adopt you into his family. What a blessing!

Ephesians 1:5–6 *"In love he predestined us for adoption to sonship through Jesus Christ, in accordance with his pleasure and will—to the praise of his glorious grace, which he has freely given us in the One he loves."*

Jesus, God in human form, came down to earth and paid the penalty for your sin, so that you can be a child of God, adopted into his family. The *glorious grace* refers to the undeserving favor God showed us when Jesus died for our sins.

Ephesians 1:7 *"In him we have redemption through his blood, the forgiveness of sins, in accordance with the riches of God's grace"*

You have redemption and forgiveness of sins through his blood, not through your works. In Jesus, God shows you that his grace covers all your sins (past, present, and future) and the unmerited favor covers any bad deed you have ever done.

Ephesians 1:8 *"that he lavished on us. With all wisdom and understanding,"*

God didn't just sprinkle some favor your way, he *lavished* it on you. In Jesus, God literally came to earth in human form to pay for our sins. Our generous Lord paid the debt that we could never pay on our own.

Ephesians 1:9 *"he made known to us the mystery of his will according to his good pleasure, which he purposed in Christ,"*

God wants a relationship with us because he is a relational God, and it gives him good pleasure to be good to us. If that doesn't make your heart explode with joy, I don't know what will!

Ephesians 1:10 *"to be put into effect when the times reach their fulfillment—to bring unity to all things in heaven and on earth under Christ."*

Through our Lord and Savior Jesus, God united us to himself.

Ephesians 1:11 *"In him we were also chosen, having been predestined according to the plan of him who works out everything in conformity with the purpose of his will,"*

Before you were ever born, God knew you would become his. If you look back on your life, you will see how God was using circumstances along the way to draw you to him.

Ephesians 1:12 *"in order that we, who were the first to put our hope in Christ, might be for the praise of his glory."*

After Jesus was crucified and ascended to heaven, God used Jewish believers in Jesus (including Paul, who wrote the book of Ephesians) to spread the gospel to the Gentiles, which includes you and me. This accomplished God's plan to unite us to him as his children.

Ephesians 1:13 *"And you also were included in Christ when you heard the message of truth, the gospel of your salvation. When you believed, you were marked in him with a seal, the promised Holy Spirit,"*

When you gave your life to Jesus, you became spiritually alive, and the proof of that is God's Holy Spirit living inside of you.

Ephesians 1:14 *"who is a deposit guaranteeing our inheritance until the redemption of those who are God's possession—to the praise of his glory."*

As we discussed earlier in the book, God gave you the Holy Spirit to sustain you through this life until he calls you into your everlasting home with him.

Ephesians 1:15 *"For this reason, ever since I heard about your faith in the Lord Jesus and your love for all God's people,"*

Our faith in Jesus Christ and our love for God's people go hand in hand. The Holy Spirit encourages our faith and sustains us there in the hard times. The Holy Spirit also enables us to love God's people and to encourage them in their time of need.

Ephesians 1:16 *"I have not stopped giving thanks for you, remembering you in my prayers."*

Seeing our walk in Jesus can be a source of encouragement and hope for other people. Don't ever underestimate how God is using you as you walk in a relationship with him.

Ephesians 1:17 *"I keep asking that the God of our Lord Jesus Christ, the glorious Father, may give you the Spirit of wisdom and revelation, so that you may know him better."*

God will never be the type of Father who withholds himself from you. If you seek his face, he will reveal himself to you. The more you seek him, the more you will get to know him. God will not give you a little piece of the Holy Spirit and your pastor a large slab of the Holy Spirit. That's not how God works. God will be as close to you as you want him to be.

I know that this concept is almost incomprehensible to grasp, especially coming from an Islamic system where Allah was so distant. Remember, God's character was distorted in Islam. The true nature of God is so giving and so generous. He is relational and wants closeness with you, a closeness that could only be achieved through Jesus. And now that you have given your life to Jesus and have received him as your Lord and Savior, the sky's the limit to how close you can be with God as your Father, through the Holy Spirit.

Ephesians 1:18 *"I pray that the eyes of your heart may be enlightened in order that you may know the hope to which he has called you, the riches of his glorious inheritance in his holy people,"*

As you draw close to God, his Holy Spirit will open your eyes to your true identity in Christ, and he will enable you to walk in your identity.

Ephesians 1:19 *"and his incomparably great power for us who believe. That power is the same as the mighty strength"*

Your ability to live your life according to your identity in Christ is accomplished by God's transforming power that is at work within you. The longer you walk with God and get to know him better, the more you'll start to see that certain things you used to do that were destructive to your life, you're no longer interested in doing. You'll also find that your life will display the fruit of the Spirit: love, joy, peace, patience, kindness, goodness, faithfulness, gentleness, and self-control (Galatians 5:22–23).

Ephesians 1:20 *"he exerted when he raised Christ from the dead and seated him at his right hand in the heavenly realms,"*

The miraculous transformation that takes place in your life is accomplished by God himself through the Holy Spirit who is with you right now, even as you're reading this.

Ephesians 1:21 *"far above all rule and authority, power and dominion, and every name that is invoked, not only in the present age but also in the one to come."*

God's power that is at work in you is the ultimate sovereign power ever. Your heavenly Father, Jesus, and the Holy Spirit hold the ultimate power and authority over everything that has ever existed, and everything that will ever exist.

Ephesians 1:22 *"And God placed all things under his feet and appointed him to be head over everything for the church,"*

Jesus is the CEO of the church—not the pastor, not the deacon, or an elder at your church. Growing up in Islam, you elevated the mosque leader in your mind because you thought he was closer to Allah. That concept does not apply in Christianity. Your pastor's role is to lead you in the faith. But don't ever mistake your pastor for the Great Shepherd, who is Jesus Christ alone!

Ephesians 1:23 *"which is his body, the fullness of him who fills everything in every way."*

Another name for the church is "the body of Christ" and you will sometimes hear this term used in sermons or conversation. Everything that is preached at your church must point to Jesus. Everything you live for must point to Jesus. Everything you're known for must point to Jesus.

God saved you because he is the most loving, merciful, gracious Person you will ever know. As you see from Ephesians 1, God chose you before the foundation of the world, not based on your merit, but because he is good. God adopted you as his own child and put his Holy Spirit in you to guide you every single day of your life until he calls you home with him for eternity.

Your Identity in Christ

But to all who did receive him, who believed in his name,
he gave the right to become children of God.

John 1:12 ESV

Growing up in Islam, your sense of identity is very much tied to your family of origin: your ancestry, your blood relatives, and where you came from biologically. There's so much emphasis on your blood ties that Islam prohibits ever severing family relationships. For example, there is a hadith in which Muhammad said, "The one who severs his blood family ties will not enter Paradise."[10] As a Muslim, you believed you were born Muslim because it was the will of Allah, and that you would die Muslim because your heritage dictated your identity.

The truth is, your identity is defined by the One who made you: God. You were born spiritually dead (as was everyone). When you received Jesus as your Lord and Savior, God put his Holy Spirit in you. Then your spirit became alive, marking you as his child, restoring your identity to God's original design. When you were Muslim, your identity was built upon your ancestry. As a Christian, your identity is built upon your Savior, Jesus Christ.

Just as any newborn baby must be nurtured day after day, understanding your new identity in Jesus can only be accomplished by drawing close to your heavenly Father and allowing him to introduce you to who you are in him. This is done by spending time with God and spending time in his Word. The amazing thing about God is that he is alive, and the Holy Spirit he put within you is alive. God's Word is also alive (see Hebrews 4:12). Since you serve a living God who wants a relationship with you, you'll be able to go for a walk and talk with God. When you have questions about a decision, you're able to ask God (as it says to do in James 1:5). As you develop your relationship with God, lean into him, and seek him and his ways, you will begin the process described in Romans 12:2: *"Be transformed by the renewing of your mind. Then you will be able to test and approve what God's will is—his good, pleasing and perfect will."*

Putting our identity in anything but God is part of man's fallen nature. When Jesus came, he freed you from bondage to sin. In John 8:36, Jesus promises that *"whom the Son sets free is free indeed."*

Since you belong to God now, your identity is found in him. As you spend time with your heavenly Father, he will show you his desires for your life. You will find it surprising how God is relational, how much he pursues you, and just how much he cares about the details of your life.

Coming from a religion where Allah was so distant and your relationship with him was so transactional, you will find that the one true God is just the opposite. As God's child, your "headquarters" has been restored to heaven, meaning that you now report to heaven, not to your parents. Your first line of communication is your heavenly Father—not your parents, and not even your spouse. Your other relationships are still important, but God has to be number one because only he is worthy of that spot. He is the One who made you and redeemed you.

Am I saying you shouldn't ask people for advice? No! The Bible encourages seeking counsel. I am saying you must protect your "God spot" with everything you have, especially if you were raised in an Islamic household, where your tendency is to go to your parents for approval. It may take months or even years to recalibrate and renew your mind to seek your heavenly Father first.

Remember, as God's child, you have access to him anytime (Hebrews 4:16). You don't need to go through bathing rituals before you can talk with God. You no longer have to wait for special holidays for God to incline his ear to you. You no longer need to strive to gain or maintain God's favor. God loves you completely.

Your New Identity

The following is a list of scriptures followed by comments that describe your identity as a child of God.

You are made in the image of God.

"So God created mankind in his own image, in the image of God he created them; male and female he created them" (Genesis 1:27).

Growing up, were you ever told, "You have your dad's eyes" or "You act just like your mom"? When God made Adam and Eve, he created them to reflect his attributes. The same goes for you. When God made you, he put some of his attributes in you, such as creativity, personality, self-awareness, a capacity for justice, truth, mercy, love, communication, spiritual perception, and relationships. You are a bearer of God's image. You reflect God's glory. For example, when you show compassion, you are reflecting God's compassion toward people and are imitating Jesus. The closer you walk with God, the more you will find yourself reflecting his attributes and cultivating the fruit of the Holy Spirit.

You are part of God's household.

"You are no longer foreigners and strangers, but fellow citizens with God's people and also members of his household" (Ephesians 2:19).

As God's child, you are fully loved and fully known by him. You don't have to clean up before you come to God—the fact is, you're already in his household! I can assure you, as you grow in your relationship with God, there will be things that you'll no longer have the desire to do. Things that were destructive will no longer interest you because you'll be satisfied with who you are in Jesus. In my field of counseling, I've encountered many people who made harmful decisions in order to belong or "fit in" somehow. In Christ, you are fully accepted into his home by the One who matters most, your heavenly Father.

You are loved by God.

"See what great love the Father has lavished on us, that we should be called children of God! And that is what we are!" (1 John 3:1).

Your true identity lies in the fact that God loves you so very much. God's love for you is not based on anything you have ever done, or anything you will ever accomplish. God's perfect, unconditional love for you is what enables you to walk this life with your chin up, confident that regardless of whatever comes your way, you are safe in your Father's arms.

You are chosen.

"But you are a chosen people, a royal priesthood, a holy nation, God's special possession, that you may declare the praises of him who called you out of darkness into his wonderful light" (1 Peter 2:9).

God picked you and set you apart for his glory, regardless of what your past looked like, regardless of what you've done. The most important mark that defines you is the seal of the Holy Spirit on your life, marking you as God's own child.

You have a purpose.

"We are God's handiwork, created in Christ Jesus to do good works, which God prepared in advance for us to do" (Ephesians 2:10).

Your purpose reaches far beyond your life on earth. The more time you spend with God, the more you will fall in love with him, the more you will want to tell people about him. As a Muslim, you spent most of your life trying to do good works to earn Allah's favor and stay out of hell. As God's child, God has already secured your eternity with him. God has also entrusted you to tell others about him, his love, and his redemption.

CHAPTER 11

Relationships Made New

*Your love for one another will prove to the world
that you are my disciples.*
John 13:35 NLT

As we've discussed, Islam puts great emphasis on blood relations. In fact, according to Islamic interpretations of the Qur'an, "Your primary position is your obedience and loyalty to your parents. This is the Islamic principle, and that's how you live as a Muslim. Even if it means you are uncomfortable, or it isn't really what you want, if it makes your parents happy, then that's what you should do."[11]

As a Christ follower, your relationships will look different from how they looked when you were a Muslim. Biblically speaking, the following describes the relationship priorities God intends us to have.

Your Heavenly Father

Loving God is your first priority. Deuteronomy 6:5 says, *"Love the LORD your God with all your heart and with all your soul and with all your strength."* Our allegiance to God must supersede our relations to anyone else. Your allegiance to God is not going to be like your allegiance to Allah. Because *"God is love"* (1 John 4:8), the closer you walk with him, the more you will be able to reflect his character to everyone else. The Bible is very clear that *"we love because he first loved us"* (1 John 4:19). For you to love others the way they need to be loved, God's love must first flow in and through you. It is so important for you to learn how to receive God's love. You do this by spending quality time with God and learning how to hear his voice.

Spouse

Unlike Islam, which elevates your parents above your spouse and children, the Bible focuses on creating a new family with your spouse. In Genesis 2:24, God highlights his original design for a married couple: *"That is why a man leaves his father and mother and is united to his wife, and they become one flesh."* When Jesus was explaining God's design for marriage, he quoted Genesis and followed it with this: *"So they [husband and wife] are no longer two but one flesh. What therefore God has joined together, let not man separate"* (Matthew 19:6 ESV).

God puts such a great emphasis on the husband-and-wife relationship to the point that he compared it to how Christ loved the church. He intended Ephesians chapter 5 to show that when a husband loves his wife and leads her well, and when a wife submits to her husband's leadership in love, they are able to walk in a unity that reflects God's character and his design for marriage.

Children

The Bible teaches that children are a gift from God. Psalm 127:3 says, *"Children are a heritage from the LORD, offspring a reward from him."*

As Christian parents, our main responsibility is to teach our children to walk in Christ. God has given our kids to us. Our job is to reflect God's love to them. We do this by making sure that our priorities align with God's will and that we are walking with God. If married, we must model to our kids what "becoming one" looks like. It is important that we walk daily with God and love our spouse well, because our kids will tend to treat other people by watching our behavior.

In Islam, the faith of children is determined by their parents. The two most trusted hadith collectors, al-Bukhari and Muslim, say that Muhammad taught, "No child is born except on *al-Fitra* [Muslim by nature], and then his parents make him Jewish, Christian, or Magian [Zoroastrian]."[12]

The Bible teaches that Jesus desires a personal relationship with each of his followers, based on their individual profession of him as Lord and Savior. No one should think, "I am a Christian because my parents are Christian." As Christian parents, it's important to help our children realize they are sinners in need of a Savior. When they decide to surrender their lives to the Lordship of Jesus Christ, they become born again and children of God.

Throughout Jesus' ministry, he demonstrated his love and compassion for children. In a society that looked down on children, Jesus welcomed them. In fact, Jesus said, *"Therefore, whoever takes the lowly position of this child is the greatest in the kingdom of heaven. And whoever welcomes one such child in my name welcomes me"* (Matthew 18:4–5).

On several occasions, parents brought children to Jesus or children approached him. When Jesus' disciples tried to send the children away, Jesus made sure they felt welcome in his presence:

> *One day some parents brought their children to Jesus so he could lay his hands on them and pray for them. But the disciples scolded the parents for bothering him. But Jesus said, "Let the children come to me. Don't stop them! For the Kingdom of Heaven belongs to those who are like these children."* (Matthew 19:13–14 NLT)

As a parent, one of the best things you can do is to model a relationship with Jesus to your children. Remember that children learn more by what we *show* them than by what we tell them.

Parents

Islam teaches that your eternal destiny depends on how you treat your parents. Like you, I grew up believing that my parents were the gateway to eternity with God. Islam teaches that your father is in the middle of the gate to Paradise and that Paradise is under your mother's feet.[13] So, as a Muslim, your sense of security in everlasting life lies in pleasing your parents. Having those beliefs ingrained in you from a young age makes it especially difficult to handle the conflict that will occur following your conversion to Christianity.

The Bible commands us to honor our parents (see Exodus 20:12; Matthew 15:3–6; Ephesians 6:1–3; Colossians 3:20). How you honor them will differ, depending on your circumstances. If your salvation resulted in your parents coming to Christ, or if your parents came to Christ before you did, then glory to God! You may not have much difficulty.

In ancient Israel, honoring one's parents required obedience, respect, and supporting them in their old age. The New Testament has the same expectation (see 1 Timothy 5:4, 8). Yet there are limits—parents are not allowed to kill their children, sell them, molest them, teach them crime, or lead them into idolatry or occultism. If any parent is in this category, their children must obey only the supreme authority, the Lord God.

Honoring parents like this means to love them as God does, following him as supreme. For many ex-Muslim Christians, including me, this may bring division. This does not surprise God. In fact, Jesus prepared us for this:

> Do not suppose that I have come to bring peace to the earth. I did not come to bring peace, but a sword. For I have come to turn "a man against his father, a daughter against her mother, a daughter-in-law against her mother-in-law—a man's enemies will be the members of his own household." Anyone who loves their father or mother more than me is not worthy of me; anyone who loves their son or daughter more than me is not worthy of me. (Matthew 10:34–37)

As you see, Jesus knew that following him could separate close family members. But the call he has on your life must supersede the plans of your family. As you read in the first chapter of this book, such was my case. Jesus warned his disciples that *"the time is coming when anyone who kills you will think that they are offering a service to God"* (John 16:2). Jesus knew about Islam's apostasy laws hundreds of years in advance.

So the question is, "How do I honor my parents where some distance is required, either physically, legally, emotionally, or spiritually?" I have two suggestions:

(1) Pray for them from a distance. Pray that God will open their eyes to see his truth. Jesus said to pray for those who persecute you. Pray for their salvation. Take a look at what Jesus did when he was being tortured: *"Jesus said, 'Father, forgive them, for they do not know what they are doing'"* (Luke 23:34).

(2) Love them from a distance. Jesus said to *"love your enemies,"* even if *"your enemies will be right in your own household!"* (Matthew 5:44; 10:36 NLT). Do good to them where it is practical and legal. Communicate with love and grace to whatever degree possible, without compromising your faith, safety, and the safety of others. Do not be unnecessarily brave; as Solomon wrote, *"It is better to be a live dog than a dead lion"* (Ecclesiastes 9:4 NLT).

During his ministry, Jesus' own family members doubted him. Mark 3:21 says, *"When his family heard about this, they went to take charge of him, for they said, 'He is out of his mind.'"* A couple of verses later we read,

> *A crowd was sitting around him, and they told him, "Your mother and brothers are outside looking for you."*
>
> *"Who are my mother and my brothers?" he asked.*
>
> *Then he looked at those seated in a circle around him and said,*

"Here are my mother and my brothers! Whoever does God's will is my brother and sister and mother." (Mark 3:32–35)

This statement is shocking to someone brought up believing the sun rises and sets on one's parents. Jesus' statement was not meant to be disrespectful to his family. In a culture that put great emphasis on duty to parents, he said this to show that doing God's will is your greatest priority. If you ever have to choose between submitting to ungodly parents and Jesus, your allegiance must lie with Jesus.

Jesus knew in advance that this conflict would occur. That's why he addressed it on multiple occasions in the Bible. When it happens, bear in mind that God is with you, God is for you, and his covenant with you is forever. He will never leave you or forsake you. He loves you and your family more than you could ever imagine. *"And I am sure of this, that he who began a good work in you will bring it to completion at the day of Jesus Christ"* (Philippians 1:6).

Church Family

When Jesus was dying on the cross for your sins and mine, his mother was there with one of his closest disciples, John.

> *When Jesus saw his mother there, and the disciple whom he loved standing nearby, he said to her, "Woman, here is your son," and to the disciple, "Here is your mother." From that time on, this disciple took her into his home.* (John 19:26–27)

If you're from an Islamic background and are reading this passage for the first time, you might have questions before reading further.

Why would Jesus give John the responsibility to take care of Mary if Mary had other sons?

Theologians believe Mary's husband Joseph was probably deceased at this point, and none of Mary's other children (Jesus' half-siblings) were disciples yet. Jesus left his mother in John's care out of concern for her. Jesus wanted his mother to be protected by one of his followers, and Mary would give the disciples the history of the miraculous events when Jesus was conceived. Since John was one of the twelve disciples and was physically present, Jesus entrusted her to him. In this moment, Jesus established a new concept of family for believers, that of the church family.

In Ephesians 2:13, Paul says, *"But now in Christ Jesus you who once were far off have been brought near by the blood of Christ."* In Jesus you have a new "blood family," a family whose members are related through the blood of Jesus.

After you have given your life to Christ, it is important to join with a local church or Christian fellowship. A church is not going to be a perfect place with perfect people; perfection does not exist, except in heaven. But a church family can be a safe haven where you're able to grow with others, learn more about Jesus, become more like him, and, soon enough, lead others to him.

Brothers and sisters in Christ, Jesus knew giving your life to him could cause you to cut ties with your own family—your safe haven. That's why Jesus put a great emphasis on surrounding yourself with a family of believers—your brothers and sisters in Christ—who can step in to encourage you, be there for you, and help you in a time of need.

The World

Cultivating relationships with those who don't know Jesus is tied to your purpose:

You are the light of the world. A town built on a hill cannot be hidden. Neither do people light a lamp and put it under a bowl. Instead, they put it on its stand, and it gives light to everyone in the house. In the same way, let your light shine before others, that they may see your good deeds and glorify your Father in heaven. (Matthew 5:14–16)

When you give your life to Jesus, you become a light to those who don't know him. This is one of the reasons why your testimony is so powerful. Sharing what God has done for you can inspire others toward hope in him. The purpose of *"letting your light shine"* is to lead people to him, not a way to earn approval from your heavenly Father. Remember: if you are in Christ, you are already accepted into God's family. Since you belong to him now, he sends you to share his good news of salvation to people in your sphere of influence who do not know him—yet.

CHAPTER 12

Your Purpose

For God did not appoint us to suffer wrath but to receive salvation through our Lord Jesus Christ. He died for us so that, whether we are awake or asleep, we may live together with him.

1 Thessalonians 5:9-10

In the last chapter, we talked about how cultivating relationships with people who are not Christians is tied to our purpose as Christ followers. Again, I want to emphasize that we don't earn God's love through works; that's Islam-based thinking. Instead, we are eager to reach the world for Jesus because he puts his love within us for others—those in our circle of influence, the people we work with, and our neighbors. As we discussed earlier, the Bible provides the instruction we need to lead the life to which he has called us. In God's Word, Jesus makes it clear that the way to live a purposeful life is by remaining in him.

In this exercise, we will explore your purpose in Christ, walking through the first seventeen verses of John 15, using the New International Version.

John 15:1–2 *"I am the true vine, and my Father is the gardener. He cuts off every branch in me that bears no fruit, while every branch that does bear fruit he prunes so that it will be even more fruitful."*

Our spiritual fruit as children of God is derived from Jesus. This is what he's trying to explain to us. He is the vine, and we are the branches. In other words, he is the source of our spiritual life.

John 15:3 *"You are already clean because of the word I have spoken to you."*

When you and I were Muslims, we believed that if we ate pork we were no longer clean. As Muslims we also couldn't start prayer until we concluded our washing rituals. Jesus, here, shows that cleanliness—true cleanliness—is a spiritual matter. No amount of washing can make someone clean. The only one who can pronounce someone spiritually clean is Jesus, and he has already declared us clean.

Why do Christians eat pork?

The law of Moses made it unlawful to eat camel, rabbit, or pork (Leviticus 11:4-8; Deuteronomy 14:7-8). The Qur'an forbids eating pork (2:173; 5:3), but allows eating camel and rabbits (6:145).[14] The teachings of Jesus are what Christians must follow. Jesus told his disciples that people are defiled by what enters the heart (immorality, murder, greed, deceit, etc.), not by what they eat. *"In saying this, Jesus declared all foods clean"* (Mark 7:19). Christians are allowed to eat any food, which is why ham is often served at Easter. However, if Christians have doubts about whether it is lawful, or if their eating may lead other people into sin, then they should not eat it (Romans 14:14-23).

John 15:4-5 *"Remain in me, as I also remain in you. No branch can bear fruit by itself; it must remain in the vine. Neither can you bear fruit unless you remain in me. I am the vine; you are the branches. If you remain in me and I in you, you will bear much fruit; apart from me you can do nothing."*

This is such an important aspect of your Christian life. When you were Muslim, your life was so "works" focused. Now your mission is to remain in God and get orders from your new headquarters: heaven. The only way to do God's will and live a purposeful life is by walking with God daily. For those coming out of Islam, this is a foreign concept because they were used to worshiping Allah who is so distant. But the one true God invites you into a daily relationship with him. Every day when you wake up, you get to talk with God and ask him, "What do you have for me today?"

John 15:6 *"If you do not remain in me, you are like a branch that is thrown away and withers; such branches are picked up, thrown into the fire and burned."*

As you develop your relationship with God, you want to avoid reverting to the "I need to earn God's favor" mindset. Jesus shows that apart from his life, empowered by the Holy Spirit, nothing you do in your own efforts could ever amount to anything.

John 15:7–8 *"If you remain in me and my words remain in you, ask whatever you wish, and it will be done for you. This is to my Father's glory, that you bear much fruit, showing yourselves to be my disciples."*

As you walk closely with Jesus, he will put his desires for your life in your heart. So whatever you ask for will naturally be in line with God's will. As a result, your behavior will reflect God's nature. For example, as you walk with God, he may lead you to help someone who, without God's nudging and changing your heart, you'd just ignore. By helping your friend, you are displaying the loving nature of God to your friend.

John 15:9 *"As the Father has loved me, so have I loved you. Now remain in my love."*

God's love is the best antidote to any fear and anxiety. As you walk closely with God, his perfect love casts out all your fears (see 1 John 4:18). The closer you walk with God, the more confident you are that no matter what comes your way, your eternity is secure with the

One who loves you most. The very thing you feared as a Muslim, the lack of assurance as to whether you're going to heaven or hell, has been decided for you in Christ. Therefore, what is left to fear? The Bible says that the sufferings of this present time cannot be compared with the glory that awaits us (see Romans 8:18). Whatever we face in this life is only a twinkle in comparison to what we have to look forward to: eternity with Jesus.

John 15:10–12 *"If you keep my commands, you will remain in my love, just as I have kept my Father's commands and remain in his love. I have told you this so that my joy may be in you and that your joy may be complete. My command is this: Love each other as I have loved you."*

By remaining in Jesus, you will naturally reflect his nature. People will identify you with your heavenly Father because your behavior will reflect him.

John 15:13 *"Greater love has no one than this: to lay down one's life for one's friends."*

It's one thing to tell people you love them; it's another to be willing to die for them. Jesus' love for you took this passage a step further. He died for you while you were still denying him.

John 15:14–15 *"You are my friends if you do what I command. I no longer call you servants, because a servant does not know his master's business. Instead, I have called you friends, for everything that I learned from my Father I have made known to you."*

The relationship Jesus calls you to have with him is not one of a dictator who orders his servants around. Jesus is revealing his heart to you. By dying for your sins and making you right with God, Jesus is inviting you to partake in his mission: to spread the news about the goodness of God.

John 15:16 *"You did not choose me, but I chose you and appointed* *you so that you might go and bear fruit—fruit that will last, so that whatever you ask in my name the Father will give you."*

Jesus shows you that he initiated the relationship with you when he died for your sins. When you surrendered your life to him, he invited you into the heart of his mission. Jesus knows spreading the gospel will be met with conflict. This will be especially true for you if God calls you to spread the gospel to the Islamic community. Jesus concludes by reminding you that you can ask God to strengthen you and sustain you through the mission to which he has called you. You can rest assured that his will, plans, and purposes for you will prevail.

John 15:17 *"This is my command: Love each other."*

When we walk closely in our relationship with God, we reflect his love to our brothers and sisters in Christ and to those God puts in our path. Love is the first fruit listed when describing the true mark of a child of God (see Galatians 5:22–23).

Next, let's talk about things you can do to help you walk closely with God.

Prayer

As a Muslim, you believed prayer was one of the pillars to be weighed on the scale of judgment to determine whether you were getting into heaven. You performed your prayer ritual out of obligation. When you missed a few prayers because of work or school, you were haunted by the fear of having to play catch-up on all your missed prayers. And by the time you caught up, it was time for your next prayer ritual.

As a Muslim, your prayer life was condensed into a number of rules and rituals. For example, you believed that someone passing in front of you while you prayed invalidated your prayer. You had to say and repeat certain Qur'an verses and passages for your prayer to be valid.

The washing ritual prior to prayer time was also very important. If you didn't wash properly, your prayer was not valid and did not count toward your good deeds, which was your ultimate goal.

As a child of God, one of the primary means of *"remaining in Christ"* is through prayer. When you belong to Christ, prayer is not a ritual but your line of communication with God. Think of God as that parent or best friend with whom you cannot wait to share good news. The first person you call when you have a crisis. The person you know will comfort you. The one you know has your back. The one who can't wait to hear from you. The one who has your best interest at heart, who sees you for who you are completely. God knows the ins and outs and all the intricate parts of your life. Nothing is hidden from him. He loves you and wants to hear from you and guide you.

You are not spending time with God to earn his favor. You are spending time with God because he loves you. The Holy Spirit is your divine best friend. He is God with you, and he is always with you. We spend time with God because he is the only One on whom we are to depend.

One of the most important things I want you to understand about your prayer life and time spent with God is that God should be the first "call" you make before anyone else. You don't have to wait until you have nowhere else to turn; go to God. He is there with you, and he wants you to develop a trusting relationship with him. You do so through your prayer life.

The following are examples of how you can spend time with God.

Reading Your Bible

According to Psalm 119:105, *"Your word is a lamp to guide my feet and a light for my path"* (NLT). The Bible is the living Word of God. It has the power to pierce through any lies you may have carried over from Islam and to show you the truth. This can be the truth about who you are as a child of God, about who God is, or about how you should handle a certain situation. God inspired many stories and parables in his Word to remind his people of his faithfulness. For example, you'll be able to see through God's Word how David, like in Psalms 5 and 32, expresses his struggle to God. This is so important for you to remember when you approach God with *your* struggles.

Remember, God is your heavenly Father now. He is not going to strike you down for being honest about how you feel. This is not Allah we're talking about. We're talking about your heavenly Father who loves you more than anyone ever could! Through reading your Bible, you'll find help and encouragement as you learn about the different people God called into his kingdom. You'll learn how God worked with them through their mistakes, how God was present with them through their doubts, and how God didn't give up on them. Instead, he faithfully and patiently worked with them and through them.

If you're wondering where to start reading, I suggest you begin with Matthew, the first book of the New Testament. Read through Matthew and follow up by reading through the rest of the New Testament. Once you're finished, start at Genesis, the beginning of the Old Testament. Let God lead you as you read through your Bible. If a verse jumps out at you, write it down or mark it.

In your reading, look for these four things: (1) commands to keep, (2) promises to claim, (3) sins to avoid, and (4) messages that apply to New Testament believers. Always read in context. The New Testament interprets the Old Testament, and the teaching epistles give doctrine for the church today. Many commands given to Jews living in Israel (such as circumcision, unclean foods, etc.) are not given to non-Jewish believers in the New Testament.

Journaling

As you're reading your Bible and asking God to speak to you, you may want to keep a journal where you can write letters to God or record what he is telling you. You may sense God's leading in your spirit. *"The Spirit himself testifies with our spirit that we are God's children"* (Romans 8:16).

God will talk to you through the Holy Spirit, and you will know it's him who is talking with you. God rarely speaks to us audibly. It usually feels as if someone is impressing a conviction into your spirit. Conversational prayer is how you can develop a relationship with God. It may feel weird in the beginning, but God is faithful to answer you and talk with you. If you choose to journal during your prayer time, let God's voice be louder than any distractions, listen for him and discern his comforting, gentle, loving voice.

Worship Music

Psalm 100:4 tells us to come into his courts with thanksgiving. Singing songs of praise to God is one of the best things we can do. It reminds us of how great God is. It reminds us of how big God is compared to any problems we may be facing. One of my favorite songs is "How Great Is Our God" by Chris Tomlin. In fact, since I didn't have a father-daughter dance at my wedding, I dedicated this song to God as my heavenly Father.

Talking with God Anytime

It took me a couple of months to realize I could talk to God outside of a church building. For some reason, I thought he would be more inclined to hear my prayers if they occurred inside a church. This is a human tradition I carried over from Islam and the mosque. It's not biblical. The Bible says, *"Let us then approach God's throne of grace with confidence, so that we may receive mercy and find grace to help us in our time of need"* (Hebrews 4:16).

As a child of God, you can talk to God on the way to work and from work. You can talk to God when you're folding the laundry, when you're cooking, or when you're at the gym.

Isn't it amazing that you no longer have to go through washing and bathing rituals before you approach God! Jesus said we are already clean because of the words he has spoken to us (see John 15:3). You can literally talk to God anytime and anywhere. Praise God!

Devotionals

You may want to read a daily devotional, which is a booklet or electronic guide that gives you a Bible verse for the day and follow-up questions that relate to that Bible verse. Devotionals help to develop structured habits of daily quiet time with God. There are devotionals that cover nearly every topic you can think of. If you want to try one out, just go to your nearest Christian bookstore and look for "devotional" or do an online search.

Just remember that a daily devotional time isn't a ritual; it's an opportunity to have a conversation with the living God, your Father, who loves you with an everlasting love. God will always want to talk with you, and he will never be too busy for you, no matter when or how you choose to spend time with him. You will never have to be concerned that the topic you're bringing before him is irrelevant to him. Your heavenly Father is a relational God—he loves you. He is with you. He is for you.

Fasting

In Islam, you were used to fasting in the month of Ramadan, eating no food during daylight hours, but then eating elaborate meals between sunset and sunrise. You fasted out of duty because Allah commanded it as one of the pillars of Islam. Refusing to fast or fasting improperly would anger Allah.

But Christian fasting is different. It is voluntary, not obligatory.

If you have a medical issue, such as insulin deficiency, please don't fast unless you clear it with your doctor. God desires mercy more than sacrifice (see Matthew 9:13). If there are medical or health reasons to avoid fasting, don't do it. You can seek God in many other ways.

As a Christ follower, you're no longer trying to earn God's favor; believers are already vessels of mercy and favor. But as a child of God, you may feel prompted to fast. Here are a few reasons:

(1) To seek God's will or direction about a decision. The Bible has many instances in which people sought God about important decisions, and in doing so, they decided to fast and pray. Fasting and prayer often go together.

(2) To worship God. Luke 2:36–37 talks about a prophetess named Anna, who spent her days worshiping God and fasting. She was not fasting out of obligation. As children of God, we can fast as a way of thanking God for everything he is doing in and through our lives; this is fasting as an act of worship.

(3) To seek God's presence. Jesus said, *"Man shall not live on bread alone, but by every word that comes from the mouth of God"* (Matthew 4:4). You may feel prompted to fast to seek God's face even more. An example of this would be skipping breakfast and lunch to spend more time with God. This helps you lose sight of the temporary and turn your attention toward God.

CHAPTER 13

Fruit of the Holy Spirit

*But the fruit of the Spirit is love, joy, peace, forbearance,
kindness, goodness, faithfulness, gentleness and self-control.
Against such things there is no law.*

Galatians 5:22-23

Through spending time with God, we can reflect his characteristics. These characteristics distinguish children of God from those who do not belong to him. In Matthew 7:16–18, Jesus said, *"You can identify them by their fruit, that is, by the way they act. Can you pick grapes from thornbushes, or figs from thistles? A good tree produces good fruit, and a bad tree produces bad fruit. A good tree can't produce bad fruit, and a bad tree can't produce good fruit"* (NLT).

These characteristics are often referred to as *fruit*. When we remain in Jesus, who is the vine (see John 15), we will bear fruit that resembles the vine. Jesus said a good tree cannot produce bad fruit. Therefore, as God's child, your life will reflect his characteristics, which means it will bear fruit.

The following list from Galatians 5:22–23 is memorized by many Christians and is seen as evidence of the Holy Spirit's work in our lives. I will describe each characteristic, how to perceive it, receive it, and reflect it to others.

Love

First John 4:8 says, *"God is love."* Love is at the core of who God is and everything he does. As a child of God, you directly receive your heavenly Father's love through Jesus. By his Holy Spirit, God reminds you of his love each day. As you walk with God, as you draw close to him, you'll be able to hear his voice and his daily reminders of his love for you. If you need a reminder of God's love for you today, ask God to show you. He is faithful!

Once when I was standing at church, listening to a worship song, I was sad because of a betrayal I had just experienced by a close friend. I closed my eyes and started worshiping God, and then I felt someone put their arms around me. Instantly, I felt as if I were in a cocoon of God's love. It's so hard to explain the feeling unless you feel it yourself! It was the safest, most calming feeling I have ever had in my life. When I opened my eyes to see who the person was, I realized it was my husband. After church, I described the feeling I'd had to my husband and told him it felt supernatural. My husband said, "As I was standing next to you, I felt God tell me to wrap my arms around you." I couldn't help but cry as I thought about God's unconditional love. In my grief, God knew exactly what I needed. The same goes for you. Whatever you're going through right now, God knows exactly where you are and what you need.

Receiving God's love is a prerequisite to reflecting it to others. Once you know beyond a shadow of a doubt that God loves you and cares for you deeply, you will love and care for others. This looks different for everyone. It can be in the form of checking on a friend who is going through a tough season, canceling a fun event to be somewhere else for a friend who is in need, or inviting a stranger sitting alone at a restaurant to sit with your group. As children of God, Jesus commands us to *love one another* (see John 15:17). Bearing the fruit of love means to demonstrate God's love to other people.

God's love toward us is unconditional. When we walk closely with God and experience his love each and every day, we become so deeply rooted in his love that it's reflected in our day-to-day life. In John 13:35, Jesus says that our display of love reflects the One to whom we belong: *"By this everyone will know that you are my disciples, if you love one another."*

Joy

Psalm 16:11 says, *"You will fill me with joy in your presence, with eternal pleasures at your right hand."* As an ex-Muslim, you ought to feel this verse at your core. For the longest time you walked this life, not knowing whether you were going to heaven or hell, having no certainty about your eternal destiny. Now that you belong to God, you have full assurance that you're going to spend eternity with your heavenly Father, the Lover of your soul. What more reason to rejoice?

When you spend time with God and you are in his presence, a joy comes on you, knowing you're in the very presence of the One who loves you most. Nothing else matters because you're with the One who is worthy of everything. Yet he took notice of you and chose to adopt you as his child. The joy of the Lord can be in you, regardless of your circumstances. You are able to go back to the most important things: You belong to God, and nothing can ever separate you from God's love for you in Christ Jesus.

Peace

Philippians 4:6–7 says, *"Do not be anxious about anything, but in every situation, by prayer and petition, with thanksgiving, present your requests to God. And the peace of God, which transcends all understanding, will guard your hearts and your minds in Christ Jesus."* God gave us this passage because he knows we will encounter times in our lives when it seems as if nothing is going the way we planned. Sometimes it may seem as if you're following God's will for your life, or you're doing what you believe God told you to do, yet you're experiencing chaos after chaos. You're putting out one fire after another. It's during these times when you'll be tempted to wonder, "Has God left me? Is God against me?" Please remember that God is for you. Go for a walk and tell God what's going on. Trust that he's listening to you, because he is. Trust that he cares for your every need, because he does! Finally, trust that he has you in the palm of his hand. Get in the habit of doing this and watch the peace of God that surpasses understanding encompass you. Similar to joy, the peace of God is best reflected when you can remain calm in the midst of chaos, because you know that God, the One who loves you most, is in control.

Forbearance

The Bible says, *"The Lord is not slow in keeping his promise, as some understand slowness. Instead he is patient with you, not wanting anyone to perish, but everyone to come to repentance"* (2 Peter 3:9). God's attribute of forbearance—also translated as "patience" (ESV) or "longsuffering" (NKJV)—was a hard one for me to believe about him. Coming out of Islam, I spent years believing I was one sin away from God losing his patience with me. Fearing that God was impatient with me cost me so much unnecessary internal turmoil and anxiety.

The truth is, God made you. When he chose to call you to become his son or daughter, God knew your ins and outs, and he decided by his own will to re-create you. When you make a mistake, God is not doubting his choice. When you fall, God is not shaking his head, wondering if you were the right person for the job. In those times of fear, anxiety, and doubt, God is not rolling his eyes, wondering why he adopted you in the first place. Rest assured, my friend, God is committed to seeing you through. Part of this process involves him allowing circumstances in your life to grow your faith. Then you shall see beyond a shadow of a doubt that he has you in the palm of his hand and is patient with your growth to become more like Jesus.

When we experience God's patience with us, we can reflect his patience to other people when they mess up. We can be there for a brother or sister in Christ when they fall, help them get back up, and remind them that God who began a good work in them is faithful to see it through (see Philippians 1:6). We can overlook our friend's mistake and choose to move past it.

My father-in-law passed away a few years ago. As my mother-in-law and I were walking toward the burial site, a man approached my mother-in-law and asked her to sign some paperwork about where to send the remaining bills for the funeral. As the man was talking, I felt time slow down, and my blood started to boil. I was so angry the man brought this up to my mother-in-law when she was about to bury her husband. I thought to myself, "How dare he!"

After my mother-in-law signed the paperwork, I looked at her and said, "I can't believe the audacity of that man! Couldn't he have waited one more hour?"

My mother-in-law sighed and looked at me. "It's okay. He was just doing his job. I'm sure he didn't mean any harm."

The patience my mother-in-law demonstrated that day could have only come from the Holy Spirit. The Bible says, *"Bear with each other and forgive one another if any of you has a grievance against someone. Forgive as the Lord forgave you"* (Colossians 3:13). When we remember how patient and forgiving God has been with us, we are able to show that same patience and forgiving spirit to others.

Kindness

The Bible says that God's kindness is intended to lead us to repentance (see Romans 2:4). God's kindness is what draws us to him. Think about it. How much did you look forward to drawing close to Allah? I didn't! In fact, my relationship with Allah was so transactional because of the nature of Islam and because his character was demanding and distant. I just did what I needed to do and hoped he wouldn't notice my faults. As a Muslim, I felt that as soon as I got close to meeting a certain standard, the bar got higher. I viewed Allah as a demanding drill sergeant who was never pleased with me. Our heavenly Father is nothing like that. Believing this truth took years of walking with him. The closer I drew to God, the more he opened my eyes to his loving-kindness. I pray that the same happens for you.

You were so used to a master who treated you like a worthless slave. Now you have a heavenly Father who welcomes you with loving-kindness and treats you like a son or daughter. He gives you the secrets of the kingdom, and now you have the opportunity to share the kingdom with others. You have received God's kindness, and now he wants you to reflect that kindness to one another. Life is hard enough. We have enough critics. So why not act on Ephesians 4:32: *"Be kind and compassionate to one another, forgiving each other, just as in Christ God forgave you."*

A few years ago, I was talking with a friend about God's kindness, and she mentioned that the words *kindness* and *God* were never spoken in the same sentence as she was growing up. What's sad to me is this person grew up in a Christian household. As I was talking with her, she said that she was surprised at the kindness my husband showed me. When she saw us together, he was always kind in his speech and actions toward me. I pointed out that this was a Christian virtue, and that Jesus commanded the husband to love his wife to the point of being willing to die for her. My friend was so surprised to hear this truth.

We ended up talking for over an hour. During our conversation, my friend shared about how she grew up around men who were constantly trying to assert control over her. She described her and her father's relationship as transactional. She said that her upbringing led her to believe this was what God and Christianity were about and therefore she wanted nothing to do with either. I gave my friend a few Bible verses to look up and encouraged her to read for herself about God's kindness and how Jesus elevated women in a culture that didn't. When we reflect God's kindness to one another, it not only empowers the people of God, but it gets the attention of those who don't yet know him.

Goodness

The Bible says, *"Taste and see that the LORD is good; blessed is the one who takes refuge in him"* (Psalm 34:8). God's goodness reassures us that God always has our best interest at heart. God's goodness was perfectly expressed on the cross when Jesus died for our sins. God continues to demonstrate his goodness to us each and every day.

God will allow us to go through certain trials. In those times, remember that our heavenly Father will use those circumstances for our good, as it says in Romans 8:28: *"And we know that in all things God works for the good of those who love him, who have been called according to his purpose."*

The above verse is such a foreign concept in Islam, where you and I were accustomed to viewing difficulties as forms of punishment from Allah. As children of God, now in Christ, we no longer have to fear God's wrath because it was satisfied on the cross by Jesus. Because of the finished work of the cross, we have received God's love and mercy instead of his wrath.

God is the best Father we could ever have. He is always looking after our best interest. You can be confident that when you go through difficulties, he has not left you. David wrote Psalm 23 as a reminder of God's goodness and the fact that in him, we have nothing to fear. David concluded this beloved psalm with this expectation: *"Surely your goodness and love will follow me all the days of my life, and I will dwell in the house of the LORD forever"* (Psalm 23:6).

In Christ, you can rest assured that you will receive God's goodness. As the psalmist said, *"I remain confident of this: I will see the goodness of the LORD in the land of the living"* (Psalm 27:13).

Faithfulness

The Bible says, *"If we are faithless, He remains faithful; He cannot deny Himself"* (2 Timothy 2:13 NKJV). The fruit of faithfulness is believing God is who he says he is and that he can do what he says he will do. Many times in your life God will put a promise in your heart, but what is in front of your eyes directly contradicts that promise. Remember what the Bible says: *"We live by faith, not by sight"* (2 Corinthians 5:7). I want to encourage you to keep pressing into what God has put in your heart.

When God called me into the counseling field, I could barely pay my rent, not to mention afford graduate school. God was faithful through it all. As I was preparing to start school, I applied for a number of waitressing jobs so I could support myself. Every restaurant turned me down due to my lack of experience. I was so disappointed and discouraged. Then I applied for other jobs. One day I got a call from an agency willing to train me to work with kids who were removed from their homes because of abuse and to help them with their behavior. I didn't believe I was qualified for this job on paper, but God gave me favor with my employer. When God calls you to something, he will surely bring it to pass.

Years later, my husband and I opened our private practice, and God blessed it. I called my old employer and offered her a leadership role in our company. Now she is part of our leadership team. Is God faithful or what! I can tell you story after story about God's faithfulness, and I can also tell you story after story about the trials and tribulations and doubts I faced during each time God put an assignment on my heart. I can promise you that wherever God calls you and whatever he calls you to, if you just press on, he will be faithful to bring it to pass.

Gentleness

Jesus says, *"Come to me, all you who are weary and burdened, and I will give you rest. Take my yoke upon you and learn from me, for I am gentle and humble in heart, and you will find rest for your souls. For my yoke is easy and my burden is light"* (Matthew 11:28–30).

Coming out of Islam, you are so used to the condemning voice of Allah. You're so used to having a burden laid upon you that is greater than you can ever bear. You're so used to being crushed in spirit because of the daily demands of the works-based mindset.

But Jesus already bore the wrath you couldn't bear on your own. The life he calls you to is one where he walks with you every step of the way and equips you for the work he has called you to accomplish. The Holy Spirit's voice never screams at you. His voice is a gentle whisper that guides you along the path of righteousness. And when you fall, you no longer have to worry about God yelling at you or condemning you as you did when you were Muslim.

If you are a parent, think about the time when your toddler was learning how to walk. You didn't scream at him when he fell. In fact, you clapped and rejoiced that he took that one step before he fell. You encouraged him to stand up, and you held out your arms to him as you gently encouraged him to come to you. That's your Father's heart for you even now. As you are reading this, he is gently calling you into a closer relationship with him. He is reminding you that he is with you every step of the way and that he will never leave you or forsake you.

When we experience the gentleness of God, we are able to deal gently with those who falter. We can live out grace in action. As it says in 2 Timothy 2:25, *"Gently instruct those who oppose the truth. Perhaps God will change those people's hearts, and they will learn the truth"* (NLT).

Self-control

Self-control is our ability to restrain our strength for the betterment of others. This ability is a fruit that can only be manifested through a relationship with God.

When Jesus was about to get arrested, Peter drew his sword and chopped off the arresting officer's ear in defense of Jesus. Matthew 26:52–54 recalls Jesus rebuking Peter:

> *"Put your sword back in its place," Jesus said to him, "for all who draw the sword will die by the sword. Do you think I cannot call on my Father, and he will at once put at my disposal*

more than twelve legions of angels? But how then would the Scriptures be fulfilled that say it must happen in this way?"

When he was arrested, it was within Jesus' power to petition the Father to send angels to fight on his behalf. When he hung on the cross for your sins and mine, he had the authority and power to call a legion of angels to end his suffering. It was within Jesus' ability to prove his strength and flex his authority. Instead, he chose not to, because our salvation was more important. He chose to die for us. He chose to suffer so you and I don't have to.

God may call each of us to a certain type of leadership role, whether it's parenting, teaching, a management position, or a role where we exercise power and authority over people under us. At times, we may be tempted to exercise our power to get things done. God by his Holy Spirit will then remind us that true self-control is the ability to hold our tongue instead of saying something we would later regret. We must hold ourselves to a higher level of accountability to make sure we are living out Philippians 2:3–8:

> *Do nothing out of selfish ambition or vain conceit. Rather, in humility value others above yourselves, not looking to your own interests but each of you to the interests of the others. In your relationships with one another, have the same mindset as Christ Jesus: Who, being in very nature God, did not consider equality with God something to be used to his own advantage; rather, he made himself nothing by taking the very nature of a servant, being made in human likeness. And being found in appearance as a man, he humbled himself by becoming obedient to death— even death on a cross!*

The next time we feel compelled to react out of anger or assert our power over someone in a subordinate position, may we remember just how much self-control Jesus exercised when he chose to die for your sins and mine.

CHAPTER 14

Gifts of the Holy Spirit

*His divine power has given us everything we need for a godly
life through our knowledge of him who called us by his own
glory and goodness.*
2 Peter 1:3

Now that we've gone over the importance of remaining in Christ
to bear fruit, we're going to talk about the gifts of the Holy Spirit.
These gifts are for the purpose of equipping you to do the work
he has called you to do: to build up the body of Christ. Again, the
"body of Christ" is the community of believers. Keep in mind that
God gives believers the gifts of the Holy Spirit at various times and
in differing circumstances. The Holy Spirit *"distributes them to each
one, just as he determines"* (1 Corinthians 12:11). In other words,
God will grant you by his Holy Spirit gifts you need for that period
of time.

Some branches of Christianity are skeptical of these gifts and believe
supernatural signs ended when the New Testament was completed.
I disagree, because it doesn't make sense that the Holy Spirit would
inspire Paul to say, *"Earnestly desire gifts of the Spirit, especially
prophecy"* (1 Corinthians 14:1) and endorse all the gifts that follow
if God intended the gifts to cease twenty or thirty years later. In the
book of Acts, Peter says, *"In the last days, God says, I will pour out
my Spirit on all people"* (2:17), but he doesn't add "temporarily"!

The New Testament says gifts for building up the church will
continue until Jesus returns (1 Corinthians 13:9–12), and I believe
this promise. God uses these gifts through you to help encourage,
edify, and build up the community of believers.

Let's take a look at the gifts mentioned in 1 Corinthians 12:4–10 and how they pertain to you.

Wisdom

Wisdom is the gift of making decisions that line up with God's will. If God calls you to a position of leadership, including leadership in your home, I encourage you to pray for wisdom. James 1:5 says, *"If any of you lacks wisdom, you should ask God, who gives generously to all without finding fault, and it will be given to you."*

God is a faithful Father, and he will give you wisdom beyond your years to get you through the situation you're in. You don't have to be facing something critical to ask your Father for wisdom. God cares about every detail of your life, even the small ones. He will never turn you away or shame you when you ask him for wisdom. Just the opposite: God welcomes you and your questions.

Coming out of Islam, it's normal to feel as if you're bothering God with your questions. However, your heavenly Father is not distant. Your heavenly Father wants to guide you. He knows you don't know everything. In fact, he wants you to lean on him because that's how you develop a close parent-child relationship. How else will you develop trust in his character? As he guides you and you learn to trust him, he will become your first resource for wisdom.

Knowledge

Knowledge is when God gives insight into a situation or a spiritual problem. I leaned on this gift a lot when God called me to counsel people. Sometimes my patients would explain a situation to me a certain way, but God gave me insight into the person's real issue— which at times was spiritual.

For example, I once had a patient who struggled with debilitating anxiety. Medication didn't help; prior counseling hadn't helped. I wondered if the real issue was spiritual. I prayed about my counseling sessions with this patient and asked her about her past. Her upbringing taught her that God was not trustworthy. In her eyes, God didn't have time to deal with her "first world problems," as she called them. This allowed me to share with her the true nature of God. The point is, God was the One who gave me insight about which questions to ask so I could identify the true nature of her problem.

Faith

Faith is the gift of trusting God, regardless of the situation. Everyone has struggled with faith at one point in their lives. Even the disciples who walked with Jesus struggled with faith. When Jesus called his disciples, they left their fishing nets or tax collection booths to follow him. When Jesus called me, I left everything I knew. Still, I had to rely on God to give me more faith. I often thought, I don't know where I'm going with God, but I know I'm not going back to where I came from. The boldness in my faith was a gift God gave me for that season of life.

When you think about it, God has already gifted you with faith for you to come to him in the first place (see Ephesians 2:8). You and I didn't just wake up and say, "Oh, I think I need to follow God." He called us and equipped us with the measure of faith needed to answer his call. As God calls you to step into new missions for him, he will give you the faith you need to sustain you. Ephesians 6:16 refers to faith as a shield: *"Hold up the shield of faith to stop the fiery arrows of the devil"* (NLT). This is because faith protects you from anxiety, fear, doubt, and all the negative, overwhelming thoughts the enemy of your soul may throw your way.

Healing

Healing is the gift of God's power working to heal someone of an illness or disorder, whether quickly or slowly. Jesus' ministry was a constant parade of people being brought to him for healing, and he healed them. Jesus asked his disciples to lay hands on the sick and pray for them. There may be times when God uses you to pray for those with illness, and they will come back to you and report that they have been healed. If this happens, please be sure to shine the light back on God and praise him because he is the source of healing.

Miracles

Miracles is the gift of displaying signs and wonders that either establish or confirm the credibility of God or his Word. The gifts of healing and miracles can go hand in hand with each other. During his ministry on earth, Jesus sent out his followers to heal and to perform miracles. The Bible says,

> The seventy-two returned with joy and said, "Lord, even the demons submit to us in your name." He replied, "I saw Satan fall like lightning from heaven. I have given you authority to trample on snakes and scorpions and to overcome all the power of the enemy; nothing will harm you. However, do not rejoice that the spirits submit to you, but rejoice that your names are written in heaven." (Luke 10:17–20)

As a follower of Jesus, God may choose to use you as an instrument of his miracles in people's lives. When this happens, it's easy to get hung up on the fact that you witnessed a miracle and forget that God is the source. Miracles should never point to you, but to your heavenly Father.

Prophecy

Prophecy is the gift of declaring a message from God, which must always be in harmony with the written Word of God. There were prophetic voices in the book of Acts who were not apostles, whose messages came to pass because they were acting in their prophetic gift. Many people say they have messages from God, yet what they say does not come to pass. False prophets may pretend to have the gift of prophecy, but their real motive is to teach false doctrine, make themselves wealthy, or gain control by pretending they are closer to

God than most Christians. Prophecy is easily misused, which is why Paul warned the Thessalonian believers, *"Do not treat prophecies with contempt"* (1 Thessalonians 5:20).

As you walk with God, he may choose to use you to declare a message to somebody. When this happens, pray and seek God. If it's truly from God, your message to that person will mean something to them. For example, a few years ago, I sensed the Holy Spirit prompting me to tell a woman something. I didn't know the woman very well, and, to be honest, I was scared to deliver the message. I had thoughts like, "What if I'm wrong?" and "She's definitely going to think I'm crazy" and "What if this isn't truly God prompting me to do this?" In fact, I even prayed and asked God to have someone else deliver that message. But God didn't release me from it. So I delivered the message to the woman, and the message meant something to her. That's how the gift of prophecy works.

Another time I attended a church conference where a woman was operating in the prophetic ministry. She looked straight at me and uttered words to me that echoed what God had already laid on my heart. I received her prophetic words because she was confirming what God had already prompted me to do. If someone approaches you with a message from God, always pray that God will give you spiritual discernment. This leads us to our next gift.

Discerning of Spirits

The gift of discerning spirits allows you to distinguish whether something is from God or from another source, including the activity of a demonic spirit. In Acts 16:16–18, the apostle Paul identifies a slave girl with a spirit of divination and casts the spirit out.

This gift can include spiritual insight and a discerning heart. Someone may present you with an idea that seems good, but if it isn't from God, it may be very destructive. First John 4:1 says, *"Do not believe every spirit, but test the spirits to see whether they are from God, for many false prophets have gone out into the world"* (ESV).

Not every "God told me" should be automatically accepted. I have had people say that God told them to tell me I needed to partner with them in a business or ministry capacity. I turned them down because that wasn't what the Holy Spirit laid on my heart. The Holy Spirit leads you into all truth. The Holy Spirit knows God's will for your life, and he will never lead you in the wrong direction. If someone ever says, "God told me to tell you," you don't have to receive the message as being from God unless God has already been laying that on your heart. Also, if a spiritual message brings anxiety, go back and review the differences between the voice of the Holy Spirit versus the voice of condemnation (see the end of chapter 5). Condemnation, shame, fear, and anxiety are not from the Holy Spirit.

In chapter 5, I provided examples to help you distinguish the difference between God's voice and Allah's voice. This is something I wish someone had provided for me early in my walk with Jesus. A few months after I gave my life to Jesus, a woman approached me at church and said I had a demon that needed to be cast out. I was a new Christian. I didn't know that a person who has the Holy Spirit in them cannot be possessed by a demon. So I believed her and asked around to see if someone could cast the so-called "demon" out of me. I am thankful God provided brothers and sisters in Christ who opened their Bibles and showed me the truth of God's Word. They reassured me that what the woman told me did not agree with God's Word; therefore, it was incorrect. So, as you grow in your walk with God, ask God to bless you with the gift of spiritual discernment. God is faithful. He will do it!

Tongues

Tongues is the gift of speaking the unknown language of the Holy Spirit. When the Holy Spirit came upon believers on the day of Pentecost, the Bible says they spoke in tongues they themselves did not understand. *"And they were all filled with the Holy Spirit and began to speak with other tongues, as the Spirit gave them utterance"* (Acts 2:4 NKJV). In this case, the God-fearing Jews from other countries were given immediate understanding in their own languages, but this often does not happen.

Speaking in tongues is one way of talking to God. Paul explains, *"For anyone who speaks in a tongue does not speak to people but to God. Indeed, no one understands them; they utter mysteries by the Spirit"* (1 Corinthians 14:2). This gift is normally used for personal prayer and worship, and God may give us this way of praying when we face a tough situation and don't know which way to turn. Speaking in tongues is one way, but this word also applies to believers who do not have the gift of tongues:

> *In the same way, the Spirit helps us in our weakness. We do not know what we ought to pray for, but the Spirit himself intercedes for us through wordless groans. And he who searches our hearts knows the mind of the Spirit, because the Spirit intercedes for God's people in accordance with the will of God.* (Romans 8:26–27)

Sometimes you know what to pray for, and sometimes you don't. Paul concludes that he should do both. *"So what shall I do? I will pray with my spirit, but I will also pray with my understanding. I will sing with my spirit, but I will also sing with my understanding"* (1 Corinthians 14:15). There are times for private prayer and also times for public worship, which brings us to the next gift.

Interpreting Tongues

This is the gift of interpreting the unknown language of the Holy Spirit. Speaking in tongues occurs regularly in some churches. When this happens, Paul says that an interpreter must be present. Look at 1 Corinthians 14:26–28:

> *What then shall we say, brothers and sisters? When you come together, each of you has a hymn, or a word of instruction, a revelation, a tongue or an interpretation. Everything must be*

done so that the church may be built up. If anyone speaks in a tongue, two—or at the most three—should speak, one at a time, and someone must interpret. If there is no interpreter, the speaker should keep quiet in the church and speak to himself and to God.

According to this passage, if someone speaks in tongues to people assembled for worship, thinking they are bringing a message, they should know before they begin whether someone else is there with the gift of interpretation. If they don't know whether an interpreter is present, it's best not to start at all. The purpose is to build up and encourage the congregation, not send them away confused.

God equips us with the gifts of the Spirit to bring his will to pass. God uses us as vessels to bring his kingdom to earth. What a privilege!

You may wonder, "How do I know if I'm operating in a gift of the Holy Spirit or if I'm using a natural or learned talent?" Here is an example from my life to illustrate the difference. I went to school for counseling and became equipped with skills to use with patients. I now use these skills (both natural and learned) to understand my patients and help them. Sometimes I will have a patient who doesn't know how to explain something to me or feels too ashamed to bring something to my attention, and it's then that God sometimes gives me special insight into the situation. When that happens, I can tell that this kind of insight doesn't come from my education. It comes from God.

Now that we've discussed why we're here, the fruit we get to produce as children of God, and the gifts God equips us with at certain times, let's dive into what happens when we die.

CHAPTER 15

Life After Death

My Father's house has many rooms.
John 14:2

The Qur'an presents a stark and severe picture of how to be accepted by God. Surah 3:85 says, "If anyone desires a religion other than Islam (submission to Allah), never will it be accepted of him; and in the Hereafter he will be in the ranks of those who have lost (all spiritual good)." Surah 101:6–9 claims, "Then, he whose balance (of good deeds) will be (found) heavy, will be a Life of good pleasure and satisfaction. But he whose balance (of good deeds) will be (found) light, will have his home in a (bottomless) Pit."

When you and I were growing up, we were taught that on *Yawm ad-Din* (the Day of Judgment), we were going to stand before Allah, "the Judge." Our assigned angels will bring forth the "book of deeds" from our lives. Our deeds, good and bad, will be read aloud. Then our deeds will be placed on a scale, the left side for the bad deeds, and the right side for the good deeds. Whichever deeds outweighed the other would determine our destiny: heaven or hell.

As a child of God and a follower of the Lord Jesus Christ, your eternal security rests not in your deeds, but in the finished work of your Lord, Savior, and King, Jesus Christ. As he hung on the cross, Jesus said, *"It is finished"* (John 19:30), indicating that he fully paid the debt of sin and satisfied the wrath of God that should have fallen upon us and all of humanity. The Bible says, *"He personally carried our sins in his body on the cross so that we can be dead to sin and live for what is right. By his wounds you are healed"* (1 Peter 2:24 NLT). Jesus—God in human form—provided atonement, redemption, and reconciliation.

Coming out of Islam, there will be times when you're faced with moments of doubt about the assurance and security of your salvation, because you were so used to having to work to achieve any type of approval from God that it almost seems too good to be true.

In those times, I encourage you to read (or re-read) the story of the prodigal son in Luke 15:11–32, with the emphasis on the older brother. You see, the older brother was already a son, but he didn't act like a son. He acted like a slave, and he worked so hard to try to earn the approval of his father, not realizing that he already had it. The older brother was not happy when his younger brother returned home and was immediately welcomed back. He believed "you need to *earn* your place in this family." Look at the father's response to the older son's complaint. His father told him that what he had was already his.

The same principle applies to us. Our Father, by his grace and mercy, chose to lavish us with his love and make us a part of his family. This is not something that we earned or could ever attain. The only reason we're going to heaven is because God decided to show us mercy and grace. It is God's heart that none should perish, but that eternal life is open to anyone who wants it (see John 3:16–17).

At the cross, Jesus had an encounter with two criminals, one on each side of him. One rejected Jesus and went to hell; the other accepted Jesus as his Lord and Savior. Take a look at what Jesus said to him: *"Truly I tell you, today you will be with me in paradise"* (Luke 23:43). That man brought nothing but his profession of faith and his submission to the Lord Jesus.

God arranged that Jesus' words to the dying thief should be recorded in Scripture to remind us of the following truth: *"For it is by grace you have been saved, through faith—and this is not from yourselves, it is the gift of God—not by works, so that no one can boast*" (Ephesians 2:8–9). In other words, Islam says you have to do this and that, whereas Jesus' actions say, "I did it all for you!"

Because of the finished work of Jesus, when you and I leave this earth, we will have no qualms or uncertainty before God in judgment. Once our soul exits our body, we will enter our home in heaven, as sons and daughters of God (see 2 Corinthians 5:8). You are no longer a slave to the fear of death, because when you leave this life, you will be with the One who loves you most, your heavenly Father.

In John 14:2–6, Jesus gave his followers a glimpse of eternity:

> *"My Father's house has many rooms; if that were not so, would I have told you that I am going there to prepare a place for you? And if I go and prepare a place for you, I will come back and take you to be with me that you also may be where I am. You know the way to the place where I am going." Thomas said to him, "Lord, we don't know where you are going, so how can we know the way?" Jesus answered, "I am the way and the truth and the life. No one comes to the Father except through me."*

In Jesus, we get to live out God's plan and purpose for our lives, knowing that when it's our time to go home, our Savior will be waiting for us, to welcome us into our eternal dwelling with him—heaven—where we will be with our Father, surrounded by our brothers and sisters in the faith.

CHAPTER 16

God's Promises to You

*And now I commend you to God and to the word of his grace,
which is able to build you up and to give you the inheritance
among all those who are sanctified.*

Acts 20:32 ESV

In this final chapter, I'd like to share with you seven promises that I found essential to hold on to throughout my transition from Islam to Christianity. These promises will help you resist and combat doubt, fear, anxiety, and other Islam-based thoughts that may come at you throughout your years as a believer in Jesus.

Instead of including the verses in the book, I have put the principle and the scripture reference. I invite you to look up each passage and rewrite it, changing any pronouns to the first person (*I, me, my*) to make the application personal. I have done the first one for you as an example, with the changed words in bold. This exercise is powerful, as it helps store God's Word in your heart for your time of need.

(1) In him I have eternal life.
Ephesians 1:13–14

And I also was included in Christ when I heard the message of truth, the gospel of **my** salvation. When I believed, I was marked in him with a seal, the promised Holy Spirit, who is a deposit guaranteeing **my** inheritance until the redemption of [all] those who are God's possession—to the praise of his glory.

(2) He loves me.
Romans 8:38–39

_____

_____

_____

_____

_____

_____

_____

_____

(3) He guides me.
Psalm 32:8

_____

_____

_____

_____

_____

_____

_____

_____

(4) He is my source of wisdom.
James 1:5

_____

_____

_____

_____

_____

_____

_____

_____

(5) He gives me perfect peace.
Isaiah 26:3

_____

_____

_____

_____

_____

_____

_____

_____

(6) He will never give up on me.
Psalm 27:10

_____

_____

_____

_____

_____

_____

_____

_____

(7) He is always here with me.
Matthew 28:20

_____

_____

_____

_____

_____

_____

_____

_____

A Final Encouragement

My brothers and sisters in the faith, although I don't know you personally, I've been praying for you. I pray that as you walk with God, you will feel encouraged that you are in the presence of the One who loves you most. I pray that you will feel his presence with you. During the times of persecution, I pray that you will remind yourself that he is with you and that he is for you.

Please know that I have prayed the following prayer over you:

For this reason, ever since I heard about your faith in the Lord Jesus and your love for all God's people, I have not stopped giving thanks for you, remembering you in my prayers. I keep asking that the God of our Lord Jesus Christ, the glorious Father, may give you the Spirit of wisdom and revelation, so that you may know him better. I pray that the eyes of your heart may be enlightened in order that you may know the hope to which he has called you, the riches of his glorious inheritance in his holy people, and his incomparably great power for us who believe. That power is the same as the mighty strength he exerted when he raised Christ from the dead and seated him at his right hand in the heavenly realms, far above all rule and authority, power and dominion, and every name that is invoked, not only in the present age but also in the one to come. And God placed all things under his feet and appointed him to be head over everything for the church, which is his body, the fullness of him who fills everything in every way. (Ephesians 1:15–23)

Acknowledgments

To Sgt. Benbow: Thank you for being obedient to God, stepping out in faith, and leading me to take the most important step in my life, a step toward Jesus. Thank you for walking me through the salvation prayer when I was in the midst of confusion and despair and for pointing me toward the hope God was calling me to in Him.

To Lorene: Thank you for opening your home to me when I had no home. Thank you for being the hands and feet of Jesus and providing for me when I had nothing.

To my husband, David: Thank you for being my #1 encourager and rooting for me day and night, for encouraging me to write this book for years, and for being there for me all the way through it and beyond.

To my children, Benjamin and Eliza, thank you for modeling child-like faith to me day in and day out. May you carry the light of the Gospel to wherever God calls you.

Last, but not least, Eric, thank you for editing my story. With your expertise on Islam, it's no question that God selected you for this project. Praise God!

Appendix

What Do Muslims Believe about the Qur'an?

Muslims believe the Qur'an is the pure, uncorrupted, and unaltered speech of Allah. It was given to Muhammad in Arabic by the angel *Jibril* (Gabriel), who made Muhammad recite or repeat each word without error. The word *qur'an* means something that is recited aloud, and Muhammad learned it by direct revelation and verbal dictation.

The Qur'an exists only in Arabic and is a copy of "the mother of the book" (Q 13:39, 43:4) or a "tablet preserved" (Q 85:22) in heaven. From these verses, they conclude that the Qur'an is uncreated, the eternal Word of God before the creation of the universe. Most also believe that the printed copies of the Arabic Qur'an are exact copies, word for word and letter for letter, of the Qur'an in heaven, and that Allah has made it impossible for one word to be lost. (This is not true. There are many different manuscripts and Arabic versions.)

Muslims identify passages from the Qur'an by their Arabic titles. They don't like the word *chapter* because it suggests the Qur'an was written with one chapter building on earlier ones. It is not in chronological order at all. In place of *chapter,* they use the word *surah.* Each surah is divided into numbered verses. Surahs are arranged by order of length, from longest to shortest—except the first one, a short passage used in prayers. When Muslims refer to Al-Baqarah ("The Cow"), ayat 106, this can be interpreted as chapter 2, verse 106. Some Muslims use *chapter* and *surah* interchangeably and prefer numbers instead of names.

Muslims believe that people who hear the Qur'an recited can be supernaturally converted to Islam, even if they do not understand Arabic. This is why parents send their children to special schools to memorize the Qur'an, even though they don't know what the words mean. About 85 percent of the Qur'an rhymes, so it is relatively easy to memorize. It takes about 10 hours to recite the entire Qur'an, always in a sing-song voice with highly styled pronunciation. Reading it aloud normally, like other books, is forbidden.

Muslims believe the Qur'an cannot be translated, so translations into other languages are "not the Qur'an" but an inferior explanation of its meaning. Whereas Christians want to put the Bible into every language on earth, Muslims want people to learn Arabic so they can read and recite the Qur'an.

Finally, Muslims believe the Qur'an contains special information or knowledge about the world that prove its divine origin (for example, embryology, geology, astronomy, or mathematics), that it came to correct the errors of the Jews and Christians, and that it is the final revelation of God.

What Do Muslims Believe about the Bible?

The Qur'an calls Jews and Christians "the people of the book" (Q 2:109, 144–146, etc.), and says God gave the Tawrat (Torah) to Moses, gave the Zabur (Psalms) to David, and gave the Injil (Gospel) to Jesus. The false revelations in the Qur'an imply that God or an angel dictated something to Moses, David, and Jesus, who wrote them down. Muslims think Jesus had revelations like Muhammad did.

The contents of the Injil (Gospel) are not described in the Qur'an, so Muslims are not sure what it is. Some think the Injil was a book that is now lost, others think it represents the four Gospels, and others think it is the New Testament. A few Muslims believe the Injil is the full Bible.

The Qur'an clearly states that Abraham "was neither a Jew nor a Christian" but a Muslim (3:67). It says all the prophets of the Bible were Muslims: Noah, Isaac, Jacob, Joseph, David, Solomon, Elijah, John the Baptist, and Jesus (6:84–85). The Qur'an knows some of the stories of the Bible, but mixes them with Arabic and Jewish legends, the Talmud, false gospels, and the inventions of Muhammad. For example, the Qur'an says that Mary was a virgin (true), and that Jesus miraculously spoke from the cradle the day he was born (false). The Qur'an says that Jesus was the Messiah (true), but that he was not the Son of God (false). It says that Jesus raised people from the dead (true), but that he was not crucified or killed (false).

Muslims believe the Christian Bible mixes small amounts of truth with large parts of error. Their ideas about the Bible rarely come from reading it, but from what their parents and teachers say. According to Islam, prophets do not commit major sins, so when they read about Noah's drunkenness (Genesis 9:20–24), Lot's incest (Genesis 19:30–36), or David's adultery and murder (2 Samuel 11–12), they automatically believe this is corruption in the Bible. If Christians show them prophecies in the Old and New Testaments about the death and resurrection of Jesus, Muslims believe Paul, Emperor Constantine, or someone else must have put this into the Bible.

Muslims believe the corrupted Bible predicts the coming of Muhammad. The Qur'an says Muhammad is mentioned "in the Law and the Gospel" (7:157), so they think he is the prophet "like Moses" described in Deuteronomy 18:18. In the Qur'an, Jesus says he came "to give good news of a Messenger who will come after me, whose name shall be Ahmad" (61:6). Muslims believe that his promise to send the Comforter or the Holy Spirit to the disciples (in John 14–16) was fulfilled by Muhammad.

What Do Christians Believe about the Bible?

The Bible contains 66 books from at least 40 different authors, written and collected over a period of about 1,500 years. These books include many different types of writing: history, prophecy, poetry, law, wisdom, biography, and end-times revelation. The Bible is divided into two main parts: the Old Testament (39 books) and the New Testament (27 books). The Old Testament was written in Hebrew and Aramaic, and the New Testament was written in

Greek. The New Testament writers were disciples of Jesus from the same time, the same language, and the same country. They were eyewitnesses of Jesus, or they interviewed eyewitnesses to write their accounts of Jesus's life.

Christians believe the Bible is the Word of God, and that *"all Scripture is given by inspiration of God"* (2 Timothy 3:16 NKJV), or literally in Greek, "God-breathed." To say that the Bible is *inspired* does not mean that God or an angel told the writers each word of the Bible to write down. Inspiration is not channeling. Instead, the Bible writers exhibit their own personalities, vocabularies, and styles of writing. The Bible is inspired because the Holy Spirit used each writer's knowledge, shared memory, and personal experiences to "carry along" the writing of Scripture. The apostle Peter explains, *"For prophecy never had its origin in the human will, but prophets, though human, spoke from God as they were carried along by the Holy Spirit"* (2 Peter 1:21).

Because the Bible is the Word of God, Christians believe its teachings should shape what they believe and how they live—especially the teachings found in the New Testament. The book of Hebrews contrasts the old and the new this way: *"In the past God spoke to our ancestors through the prophets at many times and in various ways, but in these last days he has spoken to us by his Son, whom he appointed heir of all things, and through whom also he made the universe"* (Hebrews 1:1–2). In both the Old and New Testaments, *"God spoke,"* but his voice through the Son is final. Christians believe the New Testament explains and interprets the Old Testament; that the Lord Jesus appeared to Paul of Tarsus, telling him to bring the gospel to the nations; and that the teachings of Peter, Paul, John, and Jude in their New Testament writings are just as inspired as the words of Jesus recorded in the New Testament.

When the Bible is translated into other languages, the translation is still the Word of God, even though translators differ about how best to express a thought or concept. The thoughts and ideas of

Scripture can be expressed in any language. Christians encourage memorizing and reading aloud passages from the Bible in their own languages, but they do not believe the words themselves have any special influence or power. It's what the words mean and teach that make them impactful.

What Do Christians Believe about the Qur'an?

Christians who have read the Qur'an believe it is a false revelation from a false prophet. Most Christians have never read it and have no need to read it.

The Qur'an teaches half-truths or "almost-truths" about God. For example, it teaches that God created the universe, and there is only one God who is all-powerful, sovereign, and merciful. However, the Qur'an also contains lies and distortions that misrepresent God and keep Muslims from knowing God personally. It says we do not have a sinful nature, and therefore we do not need a Savior. It says salvation depends on doing enough good deeds to outweigh our bad ones. It omits God's plan of redemption to send his Son into the world as a suffering Servant to die in our place. Islam teaches that we should serve God as slaves, never aware that we could be sons and daughters of a loving Father. It teaches that we should follow the example of Muhammad instead of the example of Jesus.

Why are these distortions in the Qur'an as they are?

On a human level, they are there because Muhammad wrote according to his own prejudices and lack of knowledge. Salvation by works is accepted by many people, so it is in the Qur'an. Muhammad had never been a Christian or a Jew, and his only knowledge came from stories he heard from travelers and caravan traders. The New Testament was not available in Arabic in Muhammad's day, so his knowledge of Jesus came from conversations he remembered. Muhammad heard stories from the Jewish Talmud and Gnostic "gospels" written hundreds of years after the time of Jesus, and Muhammad put them into the Qur'an, thinking that they were part of the Bible. The Qur'an mixes stories from the Bible with Arabic and Jewish myths.

On a spiritual level, Satan is the enemy of God. Jesus said Satan is *"a liar and the father of lies"* (John 8:44). Satan's aim is to blind *"the minds of unbelievers, so that they cannot see the light of the gospel that displays the glory of Christ"* (2 Corinthians 4:4). When Muhammad first encountered Jibril in the cave, he thought it was a demon and wanted to kill himself. But his wife urged him to continue meditating and go back, so he eventually accepted Jibril as an angel of God, becoming a channel for Jibril's messages. The Qur'an is designed to inoculate Muslims against the gospel of Christ.

Christian missionaries have different approaches to using the Qur'an with Muslims. Some find ways to use it to build a bridge to present the gospel. Others concentrate on recent evidence that the Qur'an has not been "perfectly preserved" as Muslims claim. Others believe Muhammad must first be exposed as a false prophet before Muslims will listen to the gospel and consider the claims of Christ.

Notes

1 Ezzeddin Ibrahim and Denys Johnson-Davies, trans., "Hadith 24" in *Forty Hadith Qudsi* (Cairo: Dar El Shorouk, n.d.), 102. https://sunnah.com/qudsi40:24/.

2 The oft-quoted statement that "there is no compulsion in religion" (Qur'an 2:256) does not apply in cases of apostasy.

3 Ahmad ibn Naqib al-Misri, *Reliance of the Traveller*, rev. ed. (Beltsville, MD: Amana Publications, 1994), p. 595, sec. o8.1.

4 *Reliance*, p. 596, sec. o8.3–4.

5 Surah Al-Ahzab (33:36) says, "It is not fitting for a Believer, man or woman, when a matter has been decided by Allah and His Messenger, to have any opinion about their decision. If anyone disobeys Allah and His Messenger, he is indeed on a clearly wrong Path."

6 Adoption was practiced until surah 33 appeared. Muhammad desired beautiful Zaynab (wife of his adopted son Zayd), so Zayd divorced her so his father could marry her. When Muhammad's followers murmured that marrying his daughter-in-law was incest, this surah was conveniently revealed, abrogating the practice of adoption. Since Zayd was no longer Muhammad's son, Muhammad could not be guilty of incest.

7 Qur'an 50:17–18 and 82:10–12.

8 Qur'an 16:102, 26:193.

9 Touching the Qur'an during a woman's monthly cycle is forbidden by sharia in *Reliance of the Traveller*, p. 878, sec. w16.2. In fact, reciting any of the Qur'an, "even part of a single verse," is also prohibited. See p. 81, sec. e10.7(2).

10 Sahih al-Bukari #5984, Book 78, Hadith 15, narrated by Jubair bin Mut`im. https://sunnah.com/bukhari:5984/.

11 Zaid Alsalami, answering the question, "Are a man's parents more important in Islam than his wife and kids?" on an Islamic discussion forum, circa 2021. https://www.al-islam.org/ask/are-a-mans-parents-more-important-in-islam-than-his-wife-and-kids-how-should-he-balance-his-responsibilities-between-them/zaid-alsalami/.

12 Sahih al-Bukhari #4775, Book 65, Hadith 297, https://sunnah.com/bukhari:4775/. Sahih Muslim #2659a, Book 46, Hadith 40, https://sunnah.com/muslim:2659a/. Bracketed words added.

13 These sayings come from different sources and the second is less reliable than the first, but Muslim parents often quote them to their children. See Maimoona Harrington, "Heaven Lies Beneath the Feet of Your Mother" (May 10, 2020), https://spokanefavs.com/heaven-lies-beneath-the-feet-of-your-mother/.

14 *Reliance of the Traveller* identifies rabbits (j16.2) and camels (j17.6) as permissible food.